DISCOVER GOD'S PLANS FOR YOU AND HOW TO
FULFILL THE PURPOSE FOR WHICH YOU WERE BORN!

PERRY STONE

MARKED WITH
PROMISE

YOU ARE THE GENERATION THAT THE PROPHET
JOEL SAW 2,800 YEARS AGO!

MARKED WITH PROMISE

MARKED WITH PROMISE

Published by: Voice of Evangelism Outreach Ministries

P. O. Box 3595

Cleveland, TN 37320

www.voe.org

423.478.3456

Scriptures marked KJV are from the King James Version of the Bible.

Scriptures marked NKJV are from the New King James Version of the Bible. Copyright © 1979, 1980, 1982 by Thomas Nelson, Inc. Publishers. Used by permission.

ISBN: 978-0-9855372-2-7

Copyright © 2016 by Perry F. Stone, Jr.

First edition printed 2016

Printed in the United States of America

CONTENTS

YOU ARE A GENERATION MARKED WITH PROMISE

WHAT IF I told you the prophet Joel penned an amazing prophecy about this present-day generation over 2,400 years ago? In fact, two generations in history have been *marked* with a unique promise. The first was the generation who witnessed the birth, life, ministry, death, and resurrection of Christ, all of which transpired within roughly 34 years. Christ declared to those blessed individuals that the prophets who wrote about the Messiah desired to view the fulfillment of their own predictions (Matt. 13:17). The second generation blessed with a special promise that is now being fulfilled is *YOUR* generation!

During the first Pentecost following Christ's resurrection, Peter repeated Joel's prophecy (Joel 2) in this way:

> "And it shall come to pass in the last days, says God,
> That I will pour out of My Spirit on all flesh;
> Your sons and your daughters shall prophesy,
> Your young men shall see visions,
> Your old men shall dream dreams."
> – Acts 2:17-18

The potential power of this prophecy's fulfillment explains why this generation of youth is under such demonic and fleshly attacks: to bind and blind them from experiencing this promise. Part of the blame for the bondages afflicting the youth must be placed upon the previous generation which has often failed spiritually. In 1963, Christians resisted little when Bible reading and prayer were removed from public schools. Eventually, children were taught to believe the lies of evolutionary texts, including the absurdity that they were descendants of monkeys, or the myth that we emerged out of primeval, boiling swamp water which formed some mysterious amoeba that grew legs, arms, hair, and a brain. Evolution is still taught as a *fact* when in reality, the numerous *theories* are imaginative fiction, contrived in spite of numerous "missing links." In the 1970s, sex education classes were initiated; now the public schools have evolved to essentially approve fornication among kids, going so far as to teach them how to place a condom on a cucumber. The previous generation of tolerant adults spiritually slept while your rights to read your Bible freely, along with morning prayer in public schools, were stripped by the Supreme Court. And now, some twisted thinkers are beginning to make youth feel confused about the male or female God created them to be, a diabolic and demonic brainwashing scheme. In recent news, the Satanist church has begun to implement after-school programs, which they say will focus on giving students two choices: "God" or "Satan". The bottom line is this: The whole structure is messed up because the systems of this world are manipulated by the board room of hell, led by the illegitimate god of this world, Satan (2 Cor. 4:4).

When atrocities such as abortion are permitted in society, it reveals an absence of love and appreciation for human life. What begins as the death of an infant in the womb can advance to include other groups of people. We see this today with another liberal ideology called euthanasia ("Good Death"), defined as the choice of elderly or sick people to choose to be put to death. Although euthanasia is being "sold" worldwide under the guise of "humanity" and "kindness" to those suffering, we must be on guard against adopting such laws. If judges and lawyers hold the power to decide who has the right to live or die, it is they who will also decide whether people, such as the mentally disabled for example, might be considered a useless burden on society and should be killed. All life is sacred. God has made everyone for a purpose, and it is not man's job to take away the *opportunity* for each person to discover this purpose.

By removing prayer, any belief in moral absolutes has been voided. When you tell kids they evolved from monkeys, you cannot rebuke them for acting like wild apes in a classroom! The only thing that has actually evolved is faithlessness in a lost generation, bored with life, that at times appear more like zombies glued to iPhones. They often choose to participate in immoral behaviors: pickling their brains in alcohol, cutting their skin to remove the pain they feel, or turning to drugs to "self-medicate." Since Jesus would not be welcomed in most public schools, *you are the only way to bring Him into the system.* If you don't, then who will?

FYI: God has always used young people, some actually children, to fulfill His purpose in different generations. Look at the biblical youth: When the older generation became complacent, lukewarm, or backslid, some kid would always arrive to shake things up. As a teenager David was killing bears and lions; he seemed to have no fear when he came in swinging a slingshot and taking out a giant that no other adult was willing to fight (1 Samuel 17:34-36)! Joseph was a teenager when God gave him inspired dreams about his future, and his wisdom saved the world from famine. At eight years of age, Josiah became a king in Israel (2 Chronicles 34:1). It is believed that Daniel was 17 when he was placed in the king's court in Babylon (Daniel 1 & 2). Jesus was 12 when he confounded the doctors of the law at the temple in Jerusalem (Luke 2:46-50)!

Now let's go back to the opening paragraph in this chapter. God has tagged the end-time generation (which I believe is *your generation*) with a promise to experience a global outpouring of the Holy Spirit. The indicators that the promise is being fulfilled are when amazing cosmic signs in the heavens and strange signs on the earth (Joel 2:30-31) emerge at the same time of this out-pouring. Throughout history, when the Holy Spirit was released upon men, there was also a dramatic increase in supernatural reve-lation, including spiritual dreams and visions. Many dreams in the past (and to come in the future) revealed coming events, impacting individual and national situations. These revelations often carry warnings or specific instructions for the person or nation to heed and follow.

God will release this powerful *visitation*, but you must provide the *habitation* for His presence to dwell. Paul wrote, "You also are built together for a habitation of God through the Spirit" (Eph. 2:22). People often view the Holy Spirit as some form of energy or power, similar to some type of "holy electrical current," because when He is present a certain atmosphere is created wherein people can "feel" His power and anointing. There are numerous symbols and manifestations of the Holy Spirit: a cloud (Deut. 31:15), a fire (Acts 2:3), or a dove (Matt. 3:16). However, while the Holy Spirit does manifest in power, He is first a person, a member of the Trinity (the Father, the Son, and the Holy Spirit – 1 John 5:7). He is not an "it;" rather, He is a supernatural spirit being, with distinct characteristics and feelings, sent to earth to dwell with you and in you. When you begin to realize this, then your entire life, including your personal decisions, will be impacted when you consider that He is watching and is ever present. He releases righteousness, peace, joy (Rom. 14:17), nine fruits (Gal. 5:22-23), and nine gifts (1 Cor. 12:7-10). However, He can be grieved (Eph. 4:30), quenched (1 Thess. 5:19), and blasphemed (Matt. 12:31). He is also your closest friend but is to be revered, awed, and respected.

Christ called the Holy Spirit the "Comforter" (John 14:16, 26; 16:7). The Greek word for "Comforter" is *paraklétos*. It comes from two Greek words meaning "close or beside" and "make a call," which properly referred to a legal advocate who makes the calls or decisions in legal situations. The word was used among the Greeks to describe someone standing up in court to defend another person or to give evidence in a court case. Christ sent the Holy Spirit to assist in defending you against the enemy's assaults and to stand up for you when the adversary attempts to accuse you of past sins that are now forgiven. This means, *you are never alone* when you have the Holy Spirit with you.

When you are baptized in the Holy Spirit and aligned with His purposes, you will participate in some manner in this final revival, awakening, and outpouring. Despite the failures of previous generations to take a stand against ejecting prayer and the Bible from public schools, and electing leaders who have written laws contrary to the inspired Word of God, you are part of a generation that can initiate a non-violent spiritual revolution. Both John the Baptist and Jesus were viewed as non-conformists to the system and even as radicals in their time. However, their revolution was not a government uprising but a resistance to the god of this world, Satan, and his kingdom. The gospel was preached to the poor, broken hearts were mended, and captives were delivered (Luke 4:18). When Elijah stood on Mount Carmel (one true prophet against 850 false ones), he was outnumbered 850 to 1, making his odds to succeed disastrous. In reality, he was not the "minority" but the "majority", because one person with God on their side is the majority any and every time!

Considering that you have a promise to experience the final and greatest end-time outpouring, you must discover God's will for your life. God's will is often identified as your "destiny." It's used in the Christian sense as the pre-ordained place God desires you to be: the right place at the right time with the right people to fulfill His purpose in your life. Romans 12:2 indicates there is a "perfect will of God." The word "perfect" in the original Greek is *teleios*, and it means "full or complete; full grown and full age, or the completed will of God." The root word in *teleios* is *tel* and means "reaching the end." You're not in God's perfect will until you have accepted the assignment and completed it: then His perfect will has been fulfilled. As for your destiny, Christians often throw around the word "destiny" in phrases such as: "You have a destiny." "Find your destiny." "Discover your destiny." The word is currently used as though your destiny is a one-time, one-place arrival spot where you will pitch your tent for the rest of your life. Destiny is linked with a destination. The word "destination" itself conceals the idea of a destiny, a place you are destined to arrive at. However, your "destiny" is not just a place or location; it is a progressive revelation of God's will throughout your life, as there are numerous destinations. God commanded Abraham to leave the land of Ur and go to Canaan. After arriving with his caravan, a severe famine came to Canaan and the Lord said, "Go to Egypt"—another destination. He lived in Egypt until the famine was over. God then moved Abraham and his tent city to Bethel, then Hebron, then to Salem (Jerusalem) for a brief stop, then Beersheba. Next, up to Mount Moriah then back to Beersheba! In each location, there was a special visitation from God, including some places where Abraham built altars, marking the spot for his future descendants.

The key is that all of the destinations (except Egypt) were located in the land of Canaan, the main nation God sent him to and the place of his ultimate "destiny." However, within the destiny were "mini-destinies" or "many destinies," each a piece of the puzzle composing Abraham's life. Each destination complemented the God-ordained purpose of giving him and his children all of the land where he (and they) would walk (note Deut. 11:24). It is important to seek God for His will while you are young and get on the path designed for your life. Just because God has marked you to participate in His end-time outpouring does not automatically guarantee that you will always be in the will of God; if you make bad choices, they can delay or hinder you. These can prevent you from finding God's *mark* or cause you to "miss the mark." Paul taught that believers must "press toward the mark" (Phil 3:14). In this context, the Greek word for "press" means to "pursue after something to catch a prize." If we must *press,* the implication is that we will encounter resistance in life, requiring us to actively pursue our purpose and fight for the fulfillment of God's will and our destiny. In the next chapter, I want to give you 10 significant principles related to discovering God's will.

CHAPTER 1

THE LAW OF THE WILL
10 LIFE PRINCIPLES YOU CAN FOLLOW

I RECENTLY ASKED SEVERAL groups of Christian youth what was the one question that continually remains on their mind. I was amazed by the majority's similar answers: knowing what God's will is for their lives and how they would know if the Lord was actually speaking to them. How can you discover the will of God and follow through with it when there are no open doors or clear paths to guide you? And when you do feel a calling, how can you make sure the path is actually God, and not just some stray thought that was stuck in the neurons of your brain?

GOD OFTEN CONCEALS THE DETAILS

Why doesn't the Lord lay out before you in advance the precise details of His purpose in your life? Why doesn't He just reveal your entire future at age 15 so you can be at peace and float to your destination? Why doesn't He just show you the face of the person you are to marry when you are a young teenager, and then when you see him or her, you could say, "That's them!" Wouldn't it be simpler if the Lord just showed you in a spiritual dream or vision the details of your life's occupation and what His perfect will is for you? God actually explains why he *stores away* these precious jewels (or one might call them "answers to life's questions") in Isaiah 45:3:

> *"I will give you the treasures of darkness*
> *And hidden riches of secret places,*
> *That you may know that I, the* LORD,
> *Who call you by your name,*
> *Am the God of Israel."*

God takes his time to polish our futures while we spend time searching after him. It is not such an easy phenomenon to wrap one's head around, but God says that the solution is quite simple: He hides away the "bigger picture" of our lives so that He can receive the glory for working through our lives. Based on scripture, God takes the time to guide His leaders down winding paths instead of allowing them a straight shot to their destiny. (Take, for example, the story of David, specifically in 1 Samuel 21.)

In one sense *yes*, it might seem it would be easier if you could see the big picture; but in another sense, such advanced revelation *could become a disaster.* You would probably spend too much time trying to *make it happen* if you knew *what was planned to happen.* In other words, you would move prematurely when you have not been processed and before all things were in divine order. There are reasons God doesn't always reveal the details of His purpose far in advance. I call this process *"The Law of the Will."*

1. GOD'S WILL MUST BE DISCOVERED THROUGH PRAYER.

In the pattern of the Lord's Prayer, Christ taught we should pray that God would "give us this day our daily bread," and that His "will be done on earth as it is in heaven" (Matt. 6:10-11). Thus, God's will is not a one-time destination at which you "arrive," sip sweet tea as you lie in your hammock surrounded by pine trees, while listening to the latest top ten contemporary Christian hits on your new headphones. The Christian walk may oftentimes resemble *work* more than it does a *vacation*. *God's will is progressive, and it can be missed if you willfully alter the course of your life through prayerless choices.* Daily prayer maintains your focus on God's plan by asking Him to manifest His Heaven-prepared plans on earth, and to help you walk out every day in line with his purpose. His purpose is linked with simply being at the right place at the right time with the right people. Every morning, I desire that the Lord allow me to be obedient in the smallest act and tiniest point.

Speaking of prayer, there are several prayers the Lord taught in the four Gospels that we should all pray:

1. Pray that He would raise up laborers to go into the harvest to preach and win souls (Matt. 9:38)

2. Pray and be alert (watch) that you do not enter into temptation (Matt. 26:41)

3. Pray and stay alert that you are not caught off guard at his return (Mark 13:33)

4. Pray for those who despitefully use you (Luke 6:28)

5. Pray that you be accounted worthy to escape the end-time judgments that will come (Luke 21:36)

Every day you should pray, first thing in the morning, that God's "will be done on earth as it is in heaven" (Matt. 6:10), including His will on earth for you personally. Psalms 40:8 says, "I desire to do your will, O my God; your law is written in my heart." The first phase of God's will is receiving Him as Savior (for forgiveness of your sins) and then making him Lord (the owner) of your life. Following the will of God is as simple as reading the Bible and acting upon the practical life instructions that Christ laid out in the four Gospels. As a true believer in covenant with Christ, you must pursue specific lines of behavior to stay in God's perfect will. Some call these "Christian ethics;" others, "biblical command-ments; and others, "God's do and don't list." Jesus said, "If you love me you will keep my commandments" (John 14:15). The Holy Spirit will help you to do God's will daily, as it is written, "Teach me to do your will, for you are my God" (Psa. 143:10).

Daily prayer for God's will and being obedient in the basic details will lead you to the place of God's purpose for your life. Your "destiny" is not a one-time destination, but a continual pro-cess of obedience that leads to assignments. Just as pennies add up to dimes and dimes add up to dollars, our simple acts of kindness, words, and little actions of love add up to build a heavenly account that pleases the Father. In return, He releases blessing and favor, while directing your steps (Psa. 37:23).

2. GOD'S WILL IS PROGRESSIVELY REVEALED.

If God revealed everything that He has planned, we would often try to *speed up* the timing of His plans. Humans tend to have a weakness in the area of *patience*, or the ability to *wait in expectation when nothing is occurring.* For example, let's make an assumption that you are a young person who knew whom you were to marry, but you are only 14 and the other person is 17. You would probably say, "Why not marry now because it is God's will anyway?" In reality, neither of you are mature enough to handle the stresses that will come. You have not encountered enough "life experiences" to know how to respond in a crisis, and your level of "wisdom" in dealing with different personal matters has not matured. Not to mention it is impossible to "live off of love", because hugs and kisses can't pay a light bill, car payment, and apartment rent. It takes a *job* to afford all of these things.

My VOE Partner's Director, Tiffany, began praying for whom she should marry as a young girl, and from age 17 chose not to date any young men until she knew without a doubt he was the one she was to marry. She did hang out with friends but refused to date for eight years. She set high standards and refused to allow her emotions to rule her, as emotional attraction is often confused for love. At times, what youth call "love" is in reality a mix of fleshly attraction, attention, and a bad mix of "lust of the flesh" that temporarily feels good but when division comes, ends in wounded hearts.

Once in a dream she saw the eyes and hair color of the young man she would marry. His eyes were blue and his hair a sort of blonde-brown mix. Early one morning years later, the Lord literally spoke to me (I heard a clear voice) with these words: "Tiffany will marry Nathan." At that time, I knew of three young men named Nathan and I knew they were not the description of the eyes and hair she saw years before. It was years later that a blue-eyed, dirty blonde haired, 6'1" young man showed up at the ministry center. He introduced himself as Nathan, and I knew this was the man. I called Tiffany to the house and told her I'd just met her future husband. A few years later, I conducted the ceremony for Tiffany's marriage to this same man named Nathan. Using wisdom, she did not tell others what she saw years ago or what the Holy Spirit had told me, as at the time Nathan was dating a young woman, and Tiffany could have scared him off. She patiently waited for God to fulfill the word, and it happened exactly in God's timing.

God's purposes are laid out "line upon line and precept upon precept" (Isa. 28:10), as there is always a specifically designed order and flow of events. The purpose of a progressive revelation is that doing God's will always involves some form of action: acting and stepping out in faith, *doing* and not just *saying*. Most people are not great multi-taskers and can only do one task at a time. For example, God may give one piece of His plan today, another throughout the next week, and an additional piece of the puzzle the next month. If He just dumped all of His "go forth and do this" assignments at once, not only would you be overwhelmed, but most of His assignments would not get done! That's just how humans are—one thing at a time.

I have discovered that once I have completed one task or assignment, it is then I begin hearing from the Lord about the next phase. When we were born, we first crawled, then stood up and balanced ourselves, walked, and finally ran. This is the progression of physical growth, which mirrors spiritual maturity. God will not put more on you than He knows you can handle (see 1 Cor. 10:13), so perform His assignment today then rest in patience until the next phase is revealed.

3. GOD WILL ONLY SHOW YOU BITS AND PIECES OF WHERE YOU ARE GOING.

The Bible teaches "we walk by faith and not by sight" (2 Corinthians 5:7). If we always depended upon a *visual manifestation* from God (a dream, vision, or someone's prophetic word), we would be walking by "sight" and not by "faith." The act of walking, believing, and living by faith is just that...faith. Faith is the inward force to believe in what you cannot see, accept what you cannot change (knowing only God can), and placing your confidence in him to direct your walk on a daily basis. Faith must never give in to doubt and never give up in unbelief. It must remain steadfast and unmovable, despite obstacles and opposition. Walking by faith has its challenges. David's faith was challenged by a giant, but the volume of Goliath's words and the size of his stature were no match for David's faith. David's God was bigger than Goliath, stronger than his armor, and louder than his voice. To the armies of Israel, Goliath was too big to fight, but to David he was too big for the rock in his sling to miss.

You will only receive the next piece of information when you have completed the last part of instruction.

God never promotes a person past their last act of obedience. Judge things not by what we want to do and can't, but what we ought to do and don't! Obedience will take the "t" out of can't and make it a "can." Let's say you felt impressed to give a person in need twenty dollars; perhaps they needed food. Yet, you resisted, thinking you may need that twenty dollars later in the week so you "can't" give it to the person. Your lack of obedience becomes a small act of disobedience, going against what you sense you should do. And if the next day you begin praying for God to bless you financially, this particular prayer would be like a man who refused to plant seeds in his garden while claiming a great harvest in the future.

If God sees you are moving out of His perfect plan, He can create circumstances to stop you from heading in a wrong direction. I was raised in Virginia from age 3 to 18 then had an apartment in Alabama with plans to move back to Virginia after marriage. A series of negative circumstances arose, making it infeasible to move to Virginia which would also have been detrimental to the ministry. After prayer, Pam and I chose Cleveland, Tennessee. In retrospect, Virginia was my home for a season but was not to be the headquarters for Voice of Evangelism. Had I lived in Virginia, my ministry would have turned out differently and OCI may never have been built, as I could have taken a different direction. God would not have removed my call to preach and I would be in ministry but maybe not the level I am today.

You may ask, "How do I know when I get a piece of the puzzle that it's God directing me?" The answer is that you will sense "perfect peace" (Isa. 26:3). What is crazy is that this peace will be so defining that even if the circumstances seem impossible, you will be excited and at peace knowing you are headed in that particular direction! When I built OCI during a horrible economic recession, people thought I was a bit nutty because I needed twelve million dollars and no bank in town would give the ministry a loan. However, when I saw the architect's drawings I was excited, had perfect peace, and could not wait to see the facility completed. The good news is that God paid the entire facility off before we ever moved in it!

I have learned to make plans, complete each one, and then wait on the Lord for his next project or assignment. If I have too many projects, I can become bogged down with the cares of the ministry and not spend quality time in *study and prayer*, which are the two *power twins* that have birthed and maintained both Voice of Evangelism and OCI. Take each day and move one step at a time.

4. GOD CONCEALS HIS REVELATION UNTIL YOU ARE MATURE.

At ages 18 and 19, I traveled throughout eight states as a minister, driving to every meeting, and staying in the homes of church members or pastors. Since I was living at home with my parents, my biggest expenses included a car payment, insurance, gas to drive to the meetings, and any food during the journey. This doesn't sound like much, but there were times that the church offerings hardly paid the gas and food expense! If the Lord would have said to me at age 18, "One day you will need ten million dollars a year to maintain a global ministry, and you will have a staff of more than 38 people working with you," I would have been a little freaked out. Knowing me, instead of getting excited I may have said, "Not me Lord, you called the wrong number! Where is that kind of money coming from, and who are these people, and where are the buildings I need for all of this?" Yet, forty years later, this was God's plan and He has been there through every major transition, which has been smooth and exciting. I have learned not to worry about "how God is going to do something," but just to be available as the person He stands beside and does it through!

Your level of responsibility will increase with your spiritual growth and maturity. Spiritual maturity includes how we react to negative situations. Ten percent of life is what happens to us, and the rest of life is how we respond to that. I have seen people discuss owning a business when they don't even show up on time where they work. Others talk about becoming a traveling evangelist or missionary but can't get out of bed on Sunday to drive 4 miles to church. Some say they have a word from God or they are a "world changer," but they never show up to a prayer meeting, as they are sitting every evening at Starbucks drinking a latte, telling others about their prophetic word. Maturity is not just physical growth; it includes emotional stability and mental stamina by developing the fruit of the Spirit. Let me add, God never calls a lazy person into ministry; biblically, most individuals who were called were not sitting around waiting for a voice from heaven but were already busy working as farmers, shepherds, or businessmen. In the Bible an "open door" can refer to a special opportunity. It is Christ that opens and closes the door of your opportunities (Rev. 3:8). A closed door may not be closed forever but only for a season until you have become mature enough to handle the stress and pressure.

5. EVERYTHING THAT YOU FEEL IMPRESSED TO DO IS TRAINING FOR YOUR FUTURE.

Notice I did not say what you are doing now, but what you *feel impressed* to do. I was a janitor at my dad's church from the time I was 11 to 16 years old, not because I "felt impressed" to do so but because they needed someone to do a job and I needed a bit of extra spending money. I certainly had no aspiration to advance to a permanent position (cleaning toilets for some corporation for the rest of my life); although I still occasionally use my *past experience* to do some cleaning around our offices. If you are cleaning a home or working in a fast food restaurant and you enjoy it, then advance up the ladder and do what you enjoy doing. However, do not limit your future to what you see in the present, and certainly do not get stuck in a mental rut that tells you that you are stuck in the mud of boredom for life.

As another example, at age 16 after returning home from school, at times I would walk to a church where a certain minister (one of the most talented men I ever knew) spent hours laying out books and advertisements for printing in the basement of his church which housed a large printing press. It was in this setting I learned that combining printing, advertising, and marketing were effective tools to reach people with the gospel. Hanging around a creative genius motivated me to become more creative with my ministry. At age 18, I wrote and printed my own small "magazine" (actually a newsletter) and my first book, along with revival posters. I prepared an advertising packet for the revivals, mailed to churches weeks before my arrival.

Thus, the things that interested me as a youth (printing,

graphics, and marketing) have been used during 40 years of ministry to help me reach more people with the messages the Lord has given me. Having been where you are (younger in my past), and you now going where I am (older in your future), I suggest you spend quality time with the Lord and make sure to learn all you can about everything you can, whenever you can. Knowledge always qualifies a person to speak above the ignorance that is present in the same room. People do not respect ignorance nor a "lack of knowledge." God Himself warned ignorance and lack of vision cause his own people to perish (Hosea 4:6). The more you learn and know, the more valuable you are to those you work for, and the less likely you are to be given a pink slip at the job. A few times, I have desired to hire a very skilled person, who then told their employer that they may change jobs. The employer, realizing their value, then gave that person a substantial pay raise to remain on staff.

6. GOD'S TIMING AND YOUR TIMING ARE OFTEN DISCONNECTED.

You are not always ready when you think you are ready! In the Old Testament alone, fifty-three times the question is asked, "How long?" There have been times when I was confident I was in the will of God, yet wondered when the Lord would fulfill a promise He had burned in my heart. However, I also knew that for God's plans to succeed, every decision had to be enacted in God's timing and not mine. Two personal examples will illustrate this.

About 3 O'clock one morning in February 1988, I attended an all-night prayer meeting at the Zephyrhills Church of God.

Somewhere between slumbering and awake, I was lying on a front pew holding my Bible close to my chest when I heard a clear voice say "Manna–Fest." I was immediately quickened in my spirit and body as I had never heard or seen this name anywhere. The voice continued, "This will be the title of your television program." That was the strange part: I did not have a television program and had actually never been a guest on any television show. I didn't have a television studio; I didn't even own a video camera or video recording equipment! However, instead of rebuking the voice or asking the common triple questions ("when, where, and how?"), I wrote down the word, told my wife, and hid the revelation in my heart. I did not go out and purchase a building, a studio, or equipment. I left all the details (of which there were many) up to the Lord.

Shortly thereafter, I was invited to a live call-in program where I was the featured guest discussing prophecy. The interview created a sensation in the Tampa area, and the station invited me as a speaker for their fall telethon. They requested I put together some videos or cassettes (those miniature reel-to-reel tapes in use at that time) and combine them as a gift offer in appreciation for each donation to the television station. That week, the station saw a most amazing response. Word began spreading and other stations called asking for resources to offer during their spring and fall telethon seasons. After several years, income was available to build a small studio; in fact, so small that I could not stand up and had to sit to tape my teaching videos! Eventually, we outgrew the office building and built a large office complex and studio.

Twelve years later, a revelation of the Holy Spirit caused us to begin taping a weekly television program called *Manna-Fest*, first airing on a Christian station in Monroe, Louisiana. From that initial broadcast in the year 2000, we now have a telecast aired worldwide that requires distribution of 70 individual files to stations around the United States. The fact that I developed a personal relationship with so many stations for eight years before initiating my own program enabled our ministry to receive better rates and discounts. That would not have been possible without the connections we'd formed over the years. The point is, often the timing must be right in order for everything to fall into place.

The second example took place in the late 1980s. I was preaching for Dr. Lowry in Maryland when I had an unusual dream. I saw two little girls playing in a yard. One was a bit taller than the other, and the older one was speaking to me. I asked them who they were and the one said, "I am the little girl you are going to have." I asked her name and she replied, "I am Amanda." I awoke and told Pam we would have a girl named Amanda. Shortly thereafter, Pam became pregnant and, based upon the dream, I was certain we would have a daughter. Nine months later, we had a blond-haired, blue-eyed son named Jonathan. For years, the little guy was such a trooper as he and his mom traveled with me when I preached revivals in local churches, living in hotel rooms. After eleven years with no little girl, I had a strange experience one evening. I returned from a trip and was so tired that in the afternoon I laid down in the master bedroom. I was suddenly awakened by what felt like a little child's hand on my left ankle. I awoke and was a bit stunned. I didn't know how this happened but felt an urgency that God's will was for us to have another child. Pam did become pregnant, but seven weeks into the pregnancy she had a miscarriage. At first our hopes seemed dashed, as Pam was 38 years of age, and to carry a baby at that age carried risks. However, near age 40 Pam became pregnant a third time, and on August 2, 2001, I held my little Amanda in my arms, the girl I'd seen in the dream twelve years before.

Amanda could have been born earlier, perhaps in the early 1990s. However, she became a teenager at the same time I began concentrating on youth ministry and we were completing the huge OCI facility. She has become a leader among the young girls on Remnant, and to many who attend youth events. Thus, to have a daughter the same age as the teenagers I am ministering to is a great blessing and gives me wider understanding of this genera-tion. *God's timing again was perfect.* All I needed to do was to hide His Word in my heart, and follow His inspiration and direction.

The greatest example of timing was with Lazarus. In Christ's day, many Jews believed that when a person died, their soul and spirit would exit the body and linger in limbo near the corpse for three days. They believed that on the fourth day, the spirit of the departed person would be transported to either a heavenly para-dise or to Hades, a compartment also called hell situated under the earth. Jewish belief stated it was impossible for a person to be res-urrected after three days. On the fourth day after Lazarus' death, Jesus came to the town of Bethany, meeting Martha and Mary, Lazarus' two sisters. Filled with a mix of anger and grief, they were upset that the Lord waited until the fourth day to show up, as they believed he could have cured Lazarus before he died. Jesus proceeded to do the impossible: raise Lazarus from the dead—on the fourth day. To the women, Christ was late and his timing was way off, but in reality the utter impossibility of this miracle made it perhaps Christ's greatest miracle, as in Jewish eyes any resurrection was totally impossible. Thus, Christ was really "on time" (see John 11)!

You may at times pray for direction, see an opportunity and it closes, or sense a move into a certain direction that ends up going nowhere. If you are insecure, you will begin pointing fingers, blaming the closed door on others. However, the Lord reminds us that, "...my ways are higher that your ways and my thoughts are higher than your thoughts" (Isa. 55:9). Because God sits higher, He can see far into the future in front of you, and often protects our destiny by stopping connections with the wrong job, wrong place, or wrong people. At other times God will say "no" but that "no" may be only temporary, not permanent. Moses asked God to heal Miriam of leprosy and God said "No!" She had sinned with her words and was being punished. However, seven days later she was cured, as she had learned her lesson not to criticize God's man, Moses (see Num. 12).

God's timing is not ours but this is where trust must come in. He is always working on our behalf and has our best interests in mind. One of my favorite verses sums up this section:

> "For I know the thoughts that I think toward you, says the LORD, thoughts of peace and not of evil, to give you a future and a hope. Then you will call upon Me and go and pray to Me, and I will listen to you. And you will seek Me and find Me, when you search for Me with all your heart."
>
> — JEREMIAH 29:11-13

7. DON'T BE PRESSURED TO MARRY IF YOU DO NOT FEEL THE DESIRE TO DO SO.

The following biblical observation may sound very strange, as eventually most people do marry. However, have you ever heard of a eunuch? In Christ's time, a eunuch was a man who served a king or ruler, and oversaw the cares and responsibilities of the king's harem or household. At times, a eunuch was castrated to prevent him from having any sexual relations, or he may also have been born with physical defects that prevented him from having intimate physical relationships. In Matthew 19:12, Christ mentioned three types of eunuchs: those born that way, made eunuchs by others, or those who choose to live as a eunuch for the sake of God's kingdom. There are people who are naturally born to live a life of separation from the things of the flesh, including the desire to marry. Others can choose to never marry, so as to please God and concentrate on the work of the kingdom without the distractions that come with a family life. Paul did teach that if a person desires to work for God, remaining single releases them from certain cares and responsibilities marriage requires, as there will be "trouble in the flesh" (1 Cor. 7:28); or as I would say, many cares and challenges (see 1 Corinthians 7).

When Paul wrote an entire chapter in the Bible (1 Cor. 7) on the subject of being married or remaining single, he wrote during a period when Christians were being persecuted for their faith and knew the persecution could become worse. At the time of his writing, Paul was not married and suggested his readers remain the same for the sake of the gospel, if possible (1 Cor. 7:8, 27). Paul knew that once a person is married, they enter a new arena of responsibility to care for their companion and family, and this could hinder traveling, or at times, limit the ability to minister. Young people are marrying much later than they have in the past, partially to maintain more freedom to travel and minister.

I have known of female missionaries that choose to remain single from a young woman until retirement age, in order to fulfill a call of God on their lives by starting orphanages and schools in difficult areas. This includes a great woman of God named Margaret Gains, who remained single to start a school and orphanage, and pastor a church in the village of Aboud, in Israel's West Bank during 60 years of ministry! At age 14, God spoke to her and she told the Lord she would "give Him her whole heart without return and without reserve." At age 19, she began her lifetime of missions by traveling to Tunisia. No doubt, the orphans and children she raised fulfilled the "motherly" desire she carried. This is an example of a person who remained single for the kingdom's sake.

At this time, there is a small, white house on the OCI property near one of our prayer barns housing a woman 90 years of age that has never been married and remains a virgin. She was raised in the Church of God of Prophecy and assisted in raising a large family of siblings. She played the organ for her church and spent hours dedicating her time to the work of God. She has experienced a very happy and joyful life as a "female eunuch." I tease her that the reason she has lived so long is that she never had to put up with a stubborn, complaining, or difficult man in her life!

As a personal note, being a lifetime eunuch is a "gift" that most people, including myself, do not have. There is no way I could live by myself without my wife, Pam, as I need a helper and companion in my life. Yet, if you get older, find you have no desire to be married, and are fully committed to the kingdom, you are not "weird" or "odd"; never allow peer pressure to get the best of you. It is possible you will marry later in life, as your spiritual assignments may be too significant to divide between working exclusively for God's kingdom and the responsibility of raising a family. Paul taught that there were people serving the Lord in an unmarried state and this was pleasing to God (see 1 Cor. 7:7-9). Always take the time to slowly form relationships, and understand that marriage is not a necessity to have a godly ministry. If you choose to remain single for a season to conduct the work of the kingdom, in reality you have chosen a good thing, and your sacrifice will be greatly rewarded.

8. THE WILL THAT OTHERS PLACE ON YOU IS NOT ALWAYS THE SAME AS THE WILL OF GOD.

There are certain pressures that have emerged and become so ingrained in society that a person is warned failure will soon pursue and overtake them if they alter the pattern. It is traditionally accepted that once a person receives their high school diploma, upon graduation they should immediately select and attend the best college for four years in order to pursue a lifelong career. This has become the world's system: a series of forced book reading and lectures by often-liberal professors perpetuating permissive ideals on young, impressionable minds.

In the earlier days, the only way to receive a college degree was to choose a local college and live at home, or pack your bags and transfer bits and pieces of your bedroom to a college further from home. One tremendous academic advantage today is that any person can receive a quality education online in order to earn a legitimate degree. Either of these options are great if you can afford it and know this is the will of God for your life. There is such pressure to make this decision at age 18 when you may not even have the slightest clue what you want to do with the rest of your life, nor clear direction for your life's journey. The pressure of expectations placed on you by peers or family to quicken your decision so you may start your own life may loom over your head, forcing you into a path you will later regret. If this pressure mounts, take a step back and look at the bigger picture, understanding that commitment to college will affect far more than a short, 4-year term (as college often leads to student loan debt in careers that cannot cover this cost). Consequently, blindly attending college without a direction may not be wise.

The greatest challenge is that there are tens of thousands of youth that have no clue what they want to accomplish with their lives. As a Christian, this unclear path must be exposed through intense prayer and deep intercession. Your desires may change as you get older, and if you have spent four years in one area of study and suddenly need knowledge in a new employment field, more education and understanding will be required. This is why it is important to seek God and find his will early in your life, as not to "waste" time waiting until you are 30 or 40 years of age. It can be very easy to get distracted or follow trivial pursuits that will not increase your gifting. Find the perfect will of God and He will guide your steps.

Your peers desire to help you choose the direction of your life; however, if that direction is not in your heart after prayer, you must acknowledge that the will of others does not always match the will of God. From age 14 to 16, I often changed my mind regarding what I wanted to do in life. Only after an all-night prayer meeting did I receive God's plan—to step into full-time ministry. In my decades of traveling, I've met hundreds of youth whose future plans were transformed by a God-encounter.

In the early '90s, I preached a yearly revival at Christian Life Church in Baton Rouge, Louisiana. One hundred to three hundred youth were present among the crowds each night, many of them college students at LSU. The youth pastor, Rusty Domingue, hosted a weekly Bible study on campus, and most of the youth who participated in his Living Waters Ministry also attended the revival. Two young men were present, one whose father was a lawyer and another whose father was a noted professor. Both men had impressed upon their sons their desire that they follow in their footsteps. However, both of these young men received Christ, were baptized in the Holy Spirit, and accepted a call into the ministry, much to the dismay and even anger of their fathers. It took several years for the fathers to actually accept their sons' desires to become pastors. Today, one of these young men pastors a mega-church in Florida, which he started years ago with a handful of people. The other minister also organized a church he now pastors in Memphis, Tennessee, blessing the city with numerous campuses.

I am aware of several other young people who could have remained in America, having chosen from a variety of careers, working repetitious hours to make good money. However, they felt a strong drawing to a particular foreign nation, ministering to orphans and the poor. Directing an orphanage or feeding center will not make a person financially stable, will offer few modern comforts, and requires monthly support from other Christians that can be difficult to obtain; but the eternal rewards and joy of ministering to the poor make up for any apparent "losses" in income, position, or comfort.

It is important not to allow others to throw their perceived mantle of God's will over you, although it is proper and wise to receive good *counsel* from trusted people before making any major decision. Just as seasons change, career opportunities change; your abilities and knowledge will expand, and new desires will also spring up out of your spirit. As stated, a person's destiny is continually moving forward and is progressively revealed in seasons. Be willing to take the challenge of every season and make the most of it.

9. CHOOSE TO NEVER QUIT LEARNING.

Solomon, considered the wisest man who ever lived, wrote much of Proverbs and penned seven key-words found throughout this book (scholars consider this book part of the "wisdom literature" in the Bible.) Proverbs contains numerous "wisdom nuggets" for practical living that, if followed, will prevent you from falling into the enemy's traps and help you mature spiritually. Solomon wrote that the house of wisdom had hewn out seven pillars (Prov. 9:1): One of those pillars is "knowledge" and another is "understanding." Proverbs mentions knowledge 42 times and alludes to understanding 54 times. Knowledge is the *accumulation* of facts and information, but understanding is the ability to *arrange* the information in a manner which can be *applied* and used throughout your life. Knowledge comes from several sources, including life experiences, reading books, learning from teachers, and being mentored. Knowledge can build faith and remove fear.

When a person thinks they know everything about one subject, they will cease to grow in knowledge in that area. I have said that as long as an apple connected to a tree thinks it is young and green, it will grow; but the moment it feels it is totally ripe, it can turn rotten. I have over 140,000 hours of study, which includes reading, writing, and all forms of biblical and historical research. I never weary of learning, and each day I plan to learn something I did not know about a particular subject.

From a purely career perspective, when a small business or corporation initiates layoffs and cutbacks, the CEO and the Board often discuss the perceived value of each person and what impact it would make on the success of the business if that person were given a pink slip. At times, those with the highest seniority are secure, while those with lesser seniority are sent home. However, when you have valuable knowledge that will advance the success of that business, you will likely remain on staff during cutbacks. This is not always the case, but if your knowledge gives an advantage to your company, your chance to remain on staff is higher.

Computer hacking is a negative ability that causes damage to personal lives, corporations and government files, as some information must remain private. Oddly, many of the hackers are young people whom, when they are caught hacking into secure government servers, are not put into prison but are often hired by the government to help stop foreign government hackers from accessing classified information. This is an example of how their knowledge wields great power.

Psychologists have noted that for one's mind to remain active as one ages, it is good for individuals to solve puzzles and riddles, using their mind to continue collecting information. My own mother is nearly 80 at this time, and continues to work part-time at the VOE ministry office. When I told her she could retire, she replied with two comments, saying, "I can't retire because I need the money; and anyway, I don't want to retire because I want to remain active. If I just sit at home bored, I may die early!" Work should motivate you, and once you cease working your motivation will decline. In our OCI ministry is an 87-year-old woman of great wisdom and refined dignity named Beverly Finnel. Obviously, having known Beverly for many years, in discussions I've observed she has knowledge on many subjects. At age 86, I was amazed to see her sitting among 225 others at our annual ministry Mentoring Institute. I asked her why she was there, and she replied, "I want to learn more about ministry." I laughed and wondered what we could teach this precious woman about ministry as she was already a vault of wisdom and knowledge. I later discovered she reads continually and uses her knowledge to instruct others, imparting what she knows. She said she will never quit learning as learning keeps your mind alert and your spirit activated.

Gipsy Smith was a British evangelist who conducted evangelistic meetings in Britain and America for over 70 years. During his latter years, people noticed he was still excited and energetic about the Gospel and ministering the Word. Someone asked what his secret was to being so excited about God in his old age (he was in his late 70's). His answer was, "The Gospel has never lost its wonder!" He was like a child at Christmas, still fascinated at the power of the Word and the life its preaching brought to the masses. Never quit learning, as gaining knowledge and wisdom should inspire you to gain more knowledge and wisdom. If you live to be 90, be the oldest student in the room!

10. ALWAYS PUT GOD FIRST AND GIVE HIM GLORY FOR ALL GOOD THINGS.

God is not an invisible cosmic being that we honor for 90 minutes once a week on Sunday morning, then wave farewell and shout "see you later" as we rush out the church door. God is our *Savior*, meaning he has redeemed us through his blood covenant, and He is our *Lord*, a word meaning owner and master. It is our responsibility to follow and serve him and his responsibility to be our Helper and Provider. Jesus said for you to seek first the Kingdom of God and his righteousness, and all of these things will be added unto you (Matt. 6:33). Putting God first includes doing what the Scriptures teach us, or to "act upon the Word" Christ taught us to study, believing and living based on spiritual principles. We must live a life of prayer and spend time in worship.

When I say "give God glory," this is something that is expressed with the words of our mouth. Worship is what we *say* when giving God "glory" for His goodness. Glorifying God is honoring Him. There are four angelic beings called "living creatures" positioned at the four corners of God's throne, continually shouting "Holy, holy, holy is the Lord" (see Revelation 4-5). There are also 24 elders that cast down their crowns and sing songs declaring worthy is the Lamb (Christ), giving him "honor" and "glory" (see Revelation 4).

When you are willing to brag on God, He will in turn bring blessing to you. In my entire life of ministry, I have never taken any glory for myself. I have written over 60 books, have a world-wide television program, and the ministry owns 104 acres and six major facilities used for ministry. Nevertheless, not once have I ever taken credit in my heart for what God has done. I will say, "God has been good," and "God has done this," and "It's all the Lord"; God just continues to bless what He has started. Remember, God will exalt the humble (1 Pet. 5:6), give grace to the humble (1 Pet. 5:5), lift up the humble (James 4:6), and those who humble themselves will be the greatest in the kingdom (Matt. 18:4).

When the great Evangelist D.L. Moody was dying, his final words to his son were, "If God is your partner you can make your plans big." I conclude this chapter with a few words my Grandfather wrote in a small printed flyer years ago, with the title *Use Whatever You Have.*

If you have:

- A song...sing it
- An offering...bring it
- A praise...say it

- A sin...confess it
- A habit...drop it
- A worry...stop it

- A prayer...pray it
- A message...preach it
- A lesson...teach it
- A wish...express it

- A doubt...erase it
- A trial...face it
- A burden...bear it
- A blessing...share it

While pursuing your lifetime visions, dreams, and goals, use whatever you have throughout your journey, and never take personal credit for accomplishments. It was God who gave you your feet to travel, your hands to work, your mind to reason, your eyes to see, and ears to hear. Without God you could not accomplish anything. Always give him glory!

Every morning, ask God that your steps be ordered of Him, that you meet the people you should meet, and that doors of opportunity would open for you. Accept every test as an opportunity to prove God's written Word will work in every situation, and that God's promises are faithful to see you through it. As a believer, what the devil intends for evil, God will turn for good, if you are acting on the principles of His Word (see Gen. 50:20).

CHAPTER 2

KEYS TO OPENING DOORS ON THE JOURNEY

Y OU CAN LEARN so much from the experiences of others. In this section, I want to share with you what I believe are *four significant keys* that will also assist you on your path. At age 18, when I was called into the ministry, I studied men from the "Healing Revival" era that erupted in America and continued for 7 years, from 1948-1955. Out of 20 noted ministers, some died early by abusing their physical bodies, some turned to alcohol and became alcoholics, some quit through discouragement, and others left a legacy, making it to the finish line strong. In light of learning from other's successes and mistakes, I have listed four significant keys that can help guide your life.

COVENANT WITH CHRIST

There are *four major choices* you will make that are instrumental in directing your entire future. The *first* is choosing to *enter into a redemptive covenant with Jesus Christ,* which occurs when you repent of your sins and make Christ both your Lord and Savior. Your *Savior,* Christ, has saved you, and will continue to save you in the sense of setting you free from addictions, bondages, and works of the flesh. (This is also known as sanctification.) When you make Christ your *Lord,* Christ becomes your covenant partner; all He has becomes yours and all you have becomes His.

When you are converted to Christ in your youth, you stand a much better opportunity of making *good* choices and not *poor* choices. As a believer, your decisions should follow the Word of God, and if you follow Heaven's instructions, you can prevent difficulties that come from being with the wrong people at the wrong places at the wrong time.

THE PROPER EMPLOYMENT

The **second** important choice is *correctly selecting your occupation.* As you mature from a young teen to college age, your occupational dreams may be refined or change. When I was a kid, I read books about the famous illusionist, Harry Houdini, and spent time learning different types of "magic" tricks. In seventh grade, my occupational goal was to be an "escape artist!" By ninth grade, I participated in sports and had a strong desire to play football. These plans eventually changed to becoming an architect, perhaps working with my dad's brother in Ohio. One encounter with God changed all that, when the Holy Spirit dropped into my spirit on the night that I was called to preach. Remember, many choices will emerge later in life and prayer is the guiding force.

My son, Jonathan, graduated from ITT Tech. He is highly intelligent and an excellent writer, skilled in grammar and English. For several years he worked part time at a restaurant, cooking (which he did enjoy) and washing dishes (which no one enjoys). One day he came to me and said, "Dad I've made some pretty dumb choices in life and need to do better. Do you have an opening at the office?" I needed a writer, proof reader, and someone to assist in several other important tasks required to further the ministry. Writing is his *natural* gift and computers are his *taught* gift. He now uses both gifts in the ministry!

The same is true with you. Every person has a *natural gift* such as art, music, singing, writing, communicating, organizing, care giving, or numerous other gifts that you were *born with*. Then there are *taught gifts*, or gifts that can evolve through knowledge and understanding. For me, I received from the Lord a natural *gift of communication*. At age eleven, I could entertain an entire room as a "standup comic" by telling jokes. I have never struggled with fear or nervousness when standing before any sized congregation to preach. Now, I am not saying all of the messages I preached were powerful or effective, as a few times the messages (or maybe me, the messenger) bombed out. But I could always research, digging out biblical nuggets for a word to use in messages. However, my writing skills were weak, as I had difficulty comprehending English, in fact, so much difficulty that I failed numerous English classes. My brain had difficulty grasping all the laws of grammar. It took me years to learn how to create a proper flow for each subject I would write on. Today, I still require proofreaders to ensure my grammar is correct and that my writing is not just me "telling it like it is." What you don't understand *now*, you can learn *today* and use *tomorrow*!

A MARRIAGE MADE FOR HEAVEN

Your *third* significant life decision will be *finding your lifetime companion*, or as some say, "soul mate." Marriage is a holy and serious covenant that should not be entered into lightly or carelessly. There must be an understanding of the blessings and responsibilities that accompany two different people becoming "one flesh" (Matt. 19:5). In marriage, both the man and woman bring with them their family DNA blood line. They are also carrying with them the attitudes they learned by watching their parents, and a set of expectations of what married life should be like.

A humorous observation here: After I was married a bit, I became totally disgusted at the movies that showed a husband and wife waking up. The woman would always still have her makeup on, her silky-smooth hair appearing as though she had just seen a beautician. They wake up completely attentive, immediately kissing each other on the mouth. Don't believe it! In the future, your wife will go to bed without makeup and your husband's hair will look like a twisted mop in the morning; the breath from both of your mouths will be so bad that you won't be able to get within 60 inches of each other without breathing in and yelling "yuck!" All of those hours of just holding hands and cuddling will probably continue until the kids come; then you will find the new baby gets most of the attention. But that story is for another book.

When you find the right person for you, marriage is the greatest gift imaginable. My wife Pam and I were married at a rather early age (I was 22 and she was 20.) We "dated by phone," wrote letters, and saw each other only occasionally when I would travel from one revival to another. If I were to have pre-judged Pam based upon the circumstances of her mother and father, concerned that their weaknesses would negatively influence her, I would have missed God's will. Her mother, a very sweet lady, had suffered a complete nervous breakdown when Pam was a young teenager, and shortly afterward, her parents divorced. Pam and her two sisters lived with her father and their stepmother, but things did not work out well. A wonderful family in the church, Charlotte and Jerry Skelton, took all three of the girls into their home, allowing the girls to live with them. When Pam and I were married, her father lived less than 20 minutes from the church but never showed up at the wedding to give her away to me. Yet, with all of these negative issues, she remains the most amazing woman I have ever known, and continues to be as sweet as they come. She enjoys family time, is a fabulous cook, and takes great care of our home.

GOOD COMPANY ASSISTS
MORAL CHARACTER

Your *fourth* vital choice comes *when selecting your friends*. There are only two types of people in your life: the *right ones* and the *wrong ones*. The wrong ones are always pointing you down paths of rebellion, resistance, disobedience, and sin. The right ones are attempting to lead you in the right direction: into the light of the Word and the Presence of the Lord. The wrong ones will *tolerate* you and the right ones will *celebrate* you. The wrong ones will *defeat* you and the right ones will *defend* you. The wrong ones will *stab* you in the back, while the right ones will *protect* your back. Don't be discouraged if you have a pocket full of friends instead of a palace full of friends. A few good, trusted, and caring friends are better than a room full of counterfeit friends. Prior to his death, a noted minister told a ministry colleague that if by the end of your life you have maintained five very close friends who have been loyal to you through good and bad throughout your life, then you have accomplished a great feat.

I know of a heart surgeon living in California. His family was from another country, and as a young student he attempted to apply to a noted academic college to receive the degree required to become a doctor. However, his application was continually turned down. After numerous attempts, a precious African America woman (whose job was to assist African American youth in gaining opportunities to attend noted national universities) discovered his plight and went before the university board, causing no small stir. She said that if the board did not allow this young man, whose grades were impeccable, to attend and to become a surgeon, she would step down and expose their bias to the media. They capitulated and allowed the man to attend, and eventually the man went on to graduate with the highest honors. Many years later, a man was brought into an emergency room needing emergency heart surgery. This student, now an experienced doctor, performed the surgery to save the man's life. When he went into the waiting room to give the family an update, the man's wife was the very the woman who years ago had helped get this doctor into the university. The actions taken in her past would save her husband in the future! This woman stood up at the right time for a man who was not being treated fairly, not realizing she planted a seed that would one day bring a harvest—saving her husband's life.

There are people who are quiet, and shy and don't make friends easily. They tend to be reclusive in a crowd and are soft spoken with little to say. As a believer, when you see such a person you should try to reach out to them, even though they may not fit your personal checklist describing of what you like in a friend. Loneliness is miserable if you don't want to be, and feeling friendless is even more miserable. When possible, be a friend or at least someone who converses with a shy person, as often they are the ones selected to be bullied and talked down to by others, since they won't or can't stand up for themselves.

As a believer, don't just align yourself with some clique and stand idly by while someone verbally or physically assaults another person. Stand in the gap and say, "You are not going to say that about them or treat them that way." You may save a person from self-mutilation or possible depression leading to suicide with your actions, and they will always remember you for your good deed. Most of all, God will be pleased and will bless you for standing in the gap for another person.

At the same time guard your inner circles of close friends. Jesus had 12 disciples but placed only three (Peter, James and John) in his inner circle. These three were with Christ during good and bad times; in his times of "glory" (at the transfiguration) and during his "groaning" (in Gethsemane). You will learn that as you mature, some people also link up with you for either the *right* or *wrong* motives. This is especially true when God begins to open doors of favor for you. If you are successful, some may grab your coattail, attempting to ride the train of favor they see you on. This is fine if they are faithful friends or individuals who were with you from the beginning, helping you build the tracks for the train. For example, David was surrounded by 600 mighty men who faithfully followed him for 13 years, during which time King Saul made numerous attempts to kill David. These 600 warriors remained loyal to David through numerous difficulties. However, they also knew David was the next king, and if they were willing to *suffer* with him, David would allow them to *reign* with him. This is one benefit of being a true friend and remaining faithful to your Christian companions throughout your life, as you never know where they will end up or how your destinies will unite to create amazing opportunities.

FOUR TEENS AND A BIBLE

There is an interesting story of four young men, all about the same age, who grew up in the same denomination, which will show you an example of how to choose and maintain Godly friends. They are Marcus Lamb, Jentezen Franklin, Randy White, and myself. All of us had numerous things in common. We were all completely *"sold out"* to God at an *early age*. We all drank, slept, and lived the Bible. The Lord *separated us from among others*, strengthening us to live a life of spiritual boldness and separation from carnal hindrances that brought bondages to others our own age. By this, I mean that when other kids in high school were participating in drunken parties, we spent our time praying. When they were following the fads of the crowds, we were meeting with small youth groups, hungry for more of God. We all had steadfast prayer lives and lived each day in hopes of preaching and ministering to as many as we could. We worked long hours to see God's will be fulfilled in our lives.

In the beginning, none of us had any premonition or divine revelation where God was leading us. He was leading us down a path which would wind into an amazing journey into world-wide ministry. We all preached in small rural churches, revivals, special meetings, and youth camps, watching God unfurl a series of events leading us to the global harvest over time.

Jentezen Franklin left the evangelism field and was directed by the Holy Spirit to a church of about 400 members in Gainesville, Georgia. Today, Free Chapel Gainesville has outgrown two buildings and requires multiple services on Sunday to accommodate thousands in attendance. Jentezen now has campuses in California, South Carolina and Georgia. He is reaching thousands in this generation with his yearly Forward conference during the summer and has a worldwide television audience.

Marcus Lamb began preaching at age 15 and by 19 graduated Magna Cum Laude from Lee College. He began evangelizing in 20 states throughout America and conducted extended revivals. Often as teenagers we would crisscross, ministering to the same churches months apart. Eventually in 1985 at age 27, Marcus and his wife Joni built their first television station, channel 45, in Montgomery, Alabama. Years later in 1990, they moved to the Dallas–Fort Worth area in Texas, building a Christian station called Daystar. I was on the television set with Marcus and Joni in 1993 the *first night* that he pulled the power switch and introduced Daystar to the Dallas–Fort Worth area. Later, I would remain an invited guest, assisting in fund raising during numerous telethons. Today, many consider Daystar the fastest-growing Christian television network in the world.

Randy was called into ministry at 13 years of age, preaching his first message at the Church of God in Fredrick, Maryland. As a young man he would take to the streets of the inner cities, delivering box lunches to the homeless, preaching to them with a microphone after they ate. Many of the inner city teens began accepting Christ. He would (as I did) carry his big Bible to the public school where he was given the nickname "Father White." In high school, two teachers provided their classrooms for him to preach before and after class, stirring a revival among the school's youth. Randy established teams to visit the streets and prisons to minister to those in need. By age 19, he pastored his first church in Maryland. Years later, he worked on staff for Dr. T.L. Lowery at the National Church of God in Fort Washington, Maryland, working in the children's ministry and assisting Dr. Lowery. Randy eventually moved to Tampa, Florida, where he organized a new church, the South Tampa Christian Center that later became Without Walls International Church. I conducted one of his first revivals in an elementary school auditorium, when there were just 27 members. Once a building was purchased, I would minister each year at the church, watching the ministry grow to over 18,000 members and a four story ministry headquarters. They continued providing food, clothing, and transportation to countless poor and inner city children. The church had 243 outreaches and 134 churches under their covering. One of their greatest ministry resources was a Saturday outreach in the projects called "Sidewalk Sunday School," where a truck with a team pulled up. The kids watched and heard God's Word on their level. Elmer Townsend said Without Walls was the fastest growing church in America. Despite many hindrances, including family deaths, physical attacks and satanic opposition, Randy continues ministering and directing a foundation that assists cancer patients.

My first God-encounter leading to a real spiritual transformation began at age 11 at a church youth camp, where I received the baptism of the Holy Spirit on a Thursday night. My love for God immediately increased and a flickering flame was ignited which burned with a desire for more of Him. I can remember at about 12 asking my dad to let me form a Sunday morning children's church for smaller kids in a back room of the church. There I made up lessons and cut out my own small figures of Jesus and the disciples. At age 16, after sensing the call to ministry in a late night prayer meeting, I preached my first message, "After the Holy Ghost, What Then," on April 14th, 1976. My traveling ministry began right out of high school, with local church revivals extending into many weeks. At age 18, I traded my personal set of drums, valued at about $1,200 dollars (I had cut grass and raised the money to buy it), to a printer. In exchange for the drums, the printer laid out and printed 500 copies of a book I'd written, titled *Precious Promises for Believers*. This one book sparked a multi-media outreach, where I have written and published over 50 different books, as well as hundreds of CDs and DVDs, and eventually hosting a weekly television program called *Manna-Fest* that reaches into every nation of the world!

All four of these brief biographies are examples demonstrating that being faithful to God in the little things (in the times when no one knows or even cares about you and your dreams, and being steadfast and firm in your convictions) will unlock doors revealing the ministry assignments that are concealed from you at this moment.

THREE OTHER MEN IN MINISTRY

There are three men that began their 1940s ministries as evangelists in the Baptist denomination. They were Bron Clifford, Chuck Templeton, and Billy Graham. In a noted Baptist magazine, both Clifford and Templeton were named as upcoming ministers that would impact the nation. Both were young, in their twenties, and both were having large crowds of thousands attending their crusades. Oddly, Billy Graham was never named. Ten years later, Clifford and Templeton were no longer in the ministry, and their names were eventually forgotten. In contrast, now over 60 years later, Billy Graham is a legend: the evangelist who has met with presidents and prayed with world leaders, maintaining his integrity until the end. Without going into details, the other two men destroyed their potential. All of your decisions in life will either help or harm your potential. I have been aware that for over 40 years, people are always watching every move I make, especially in public: how I treat people, how I speak to my wife, how I handle pressure, and with smartphones some individuals attempt to take a picture or video anything and everything you do! People will remember your name, your integrity, and whether you kept the promises made with your mouth long after you are gone.

KEEP THE KEYS ON A KEYRING

It should come as no surprise to you that Satan (or the enemy) will do his best to close and lock the door on any of these four keys by confusing you, or by bringing the wrong person into your life. This is why you must always carry your "keyring": the Word of God. Remember: *When God desires to bless you, He will bring a person into your life; and when Satan desires to stop you, he will bring a different kind of person into your life.* People that are "kingdom connections" (brought together by God to further his kingdom) in your life are important as they can assist in your destiny. Christ commented that when we give to others or for the Kingdom of God, "men would give unto our bosom" (Luke 6:38), meaning the Lord will use men to assist in the provision of your needs. Jesus also spoke a parable about a wheat field that had been compromised with seeds that eventually grew tares, which look similar to wheat. But as harvest time approaches, the tares become obvious. These bitter and poisonous plants become dangerously intertwined in the wheat, disrupting a smooth harvest, as they can make people dangerously sick. These tares in a good field represent bad influences and wrong people who weave themselves into your growth process; instead of nourishing you spiritually and emotionally, they cling close, planting negative seeds into your spirit and eventually choking out the seeds of God's knowledge within you (see Matthew 13).

You may never recognize a *tare* when it enters your life, but the *fruit* they produce can eventually become a detrimental distraction to you. God gave Abraham an exciting *seed promise* of a natural son born to him, but because his wife was barren, she permitted him to impregnate Hagar, her servant. Later, Abraham's wife Sarah, at age 90, conceived and birthed a son named Isaac. Eventually, Ishmael, Hagar's son, mocked Isaac. Sarah, sensing future danger and confusion between these two boys, expelled Hagar and Ishmael from the property, banning the family for life. Abraham's *failure* and *promise* could not live together in the same house, just as good and bad seed cannot bring forth a pure harvest, and bitter and sweet water mixed together is undrinkable (see Genesis 16 and 21).

Sometimes it is not just the wrong *people* but also wrong *thinking*, as the adversary tries to rewire our brains to accept beliefs that, in reality, are dangerous time bombs planted to explode in the future. Samson's tare seeds were the strange women he continually flirted with, one named Delilah, a Philistine beauty queen who caught his attention and ensnared him in her seductive web, like a spider when trapping a curious fly. Samson assumed he could break his Nazarite vows and God would continue to anoint him to defeat his enemies. His eyes were opened to his mistake when a razor clipped his hair, breaking the final vow that identified him as a Nazarite. When he lost his spiritual eyes (his understanding), he eventually lost his natural eyes (the Philistines physically removed them, blinding him), and the anointing and strength was stripped from him (see Judges 14 through 16).

Walking with God and following His will is a continuous process which reminds me of when Peter walked on water. He knew it was impossible for a human to walk on water; yet, Christ told Peter to "Come," requiring faith to go to a place that was impossible in the natural. At times the Spirit of God tells us to do something that is impossible for us and only possible through him. When you step out to make the impossible possible, it is called "faith" (Heb. 11:1). If Peter had stepped out of the boat without a word from God, he would have immediately sunk. *You cannot walk on water without a word from the Lord, and we cannot see the impossible become possible without faith in God*

THE DEVIL'S STRATEGY

Just as God has a process, Satan also has a process to disrupt you as you move toward God. The *first* process is simple: to prevent a person from receiving Christ as their redeemer. Without Christ, Satan maintains his legal authority, control, and dominion over a person. They become his puppet on a string, and he manipulates their desires and movements as the puppet master. He uses *peer pressure,* which plays on your fear of *not being accepted by others,* and fear of *rejection by friends* to build a barrier between you and Christ. Satan tells you serving Christ is a hindrance to having friends, but Satan's real fear is that you will *influence* those friends to serve the Lord!

Isaiah revealed that the Messiah (Christ) was "despised and rejected of men; a man of sorrow and familiar with grief" (Isa. 53:3-4). We are told that Christ is "touched by the feelings of our infirmities, and was tempted as you and I were, yet without sin" (Heb. 4:25). The enemy wants you to think "God cannot understand the loneliness and isolation I am feeling." But this is incorrect, because God's Son, Jesus Christ, certainly does. The empty feeling accompanying rejection was experienced by Jesus. In his greatest moment of need at crucifixion, his disciples, his followers, and even the people he'd healed all fled from the scene: only his critics and mockers surrounded him. This is why he is "touched" by our weaknesses (a Greek word for "sympathy"), meaning Christ is sympathetic for you when you are struggling.

Satan's *second* process is pressure to compromise. Look at Daniel in Babylon (Daniel 1). He and tens of thousands of Jews were led from Judea to Babylon by King Nebuchadnezzar's army. Upon arriving, the king desired to train several Jewish youths in the manners and language of Babylon in order to communicate with the Jews. Daniel was chosen. He was good looking, intelligent, skilled, and was taught under Babylon's finest educators for several years. There were, however, some catches. First, Babylon was a pagan, idol-worshipping city. The king went so far as to change Daniel's name to Belshazzar, the name of a Babylonian god. Second, the Babylonians would eat meat that had been burned on altars for false Gods, something a devout Jew was forbidden to do. Third, the Babylonians threw wild parties and were heavy drinkers; it was expected that when the king threw a party, all of his administration were required to participate.

Notice how Daniel reacted. Many Christians today would say to themselves, "When in Babylon just do like the Babylonians," or "I don't want to offend these Babylonians so I'm headed to the party," or "Hey, don't blame me for drinking with the rest of them, it's part of my job!" In the book of Daniel, the prophet never once identifies himself using his Babylonian name. He always says, "I Daniel" (Dan. 7:15; 8:15; 8:27; 9:2; 10:2; 10:7; 12:5), using his Hebrew name meaning "God is Judge." He would not allow others to redefine who he was. He knew he was a Hebrew and in his heart would not compromise that fact. If you call yourself a Christian and know who you are in Christ, never compromise, back down, or be ashamed of the one (Christ) who was mocked, despised, hated, and yet still died for you.

When Daniel was first brought before the "king's table," he and three of his fellow Jews were given a hearty meal, including meat that was sacrificed to an idol and wine from the king's wine cellar. Here again, it would be easy to say, "It's just us four and we can keep this little secret among us; if we eat this steak and drink this wine, no one will actually know." This may be true naturally but not true spiritually, as the Lord sees and knows all things. Daniel was not as concerned with offending the king as he was offending God, breaking the laws and customs of his people. He requested to have his menu changed and refused to drink wine from the king's table (see Daniel 1). This could have ended up being a dangerous move that would have offended the king, sending Daniel and his companions to the king's prison. Instead, their change of diet was so effective that Daniel and his three friends looked healthier than all of the others in the king's court! God blesses non-compromising believers!

The stories of Daniel in Babylon demonstrate the tendency of the worldly group to "go with the flow" and participate in whatever is popular, even if it means sacrificing your convictions on the altar. Let me add here, I personally despise alcohol, and I have held my firm and uncompromising conviction (to never touch strong drink) since my teen years. In the Bible, no good ever came out of drinking alcohol. Noah compromised and ended up naked in his tent, with a curse being placed on his grandson Canaan

(Gen. 9:20-25). Lot was made drunk and committed incest with his two daughters (see Genesis 19). King Belshazzar drank wine from the holy vessels in Babylon, and that same night the Persians overthrew the Babylonians, slaying the drunken king (Dan. 5:23-30). Abigail's husband Nabal went on a drunken spree and died in the morning after his "heart died within him, and he became as a stone," (1 Sam. 25:37). One Biblical prophet even placed a "woe" (this is like placing a curse) on those who give their neighbor's strong drink, and warned that violence would follow them (see Hab. 2:15-17). In my home town of Cleveland, several young people, who knew better, went out with friends and got drunk upon graduating from high school. Later that morning they were involved in fatal car accidents. They were popular and admired in the community with bright futures ahead of them, but one night of compromise cost them their lives!

Even your best intention at the wrong place and time can be costly. I know of a sad situation where a precious Christian girl had several unsaved friends who would go to a bar each weekend, drink, and drive home during the early hours of the morning. One night she chose to go with them: not to drink (as she was against it), but to make sure she could drive them home safely. Early in the morning, with a carload full of drunken college teens, she fell asleep on the interstate and crashed the car. The other kids survived with only injuries, and she was the one unfortunately killed.

Having traveled across the nation for over forty years, I have stayed in pastor's homes where a son or daughter was in rebellion against their Christian values or parental instructions. On a few occasions, I saw dreams of serious danger coming if they continued in their rebellion. In many instances they rejected the warnings and later paid a serious price for their dullness of hearing and spiritual blindness, sometimes choosing to marry a person who turned them from God and from their parents.

Just because the "crowd" permits it does not make it right. As I have said, "The crowd may be walking right into hell eyes closed; does that mean you walk with them because you find the need to follow the crowd?" Some things might be legal (such as an abortion) but that does not make them right.

> God's ways are not man's ways. We must always listen to the conviction of the Spirit, and not just follow the world. Scripture says sin is fun or a season, and this season may be much shorter than you think (Heb. 11:25).

Satan's *third* process is to keep a person in some type of addiction or bondage like Samson (blind, bound, going round and round) to prevent them from experiencing freedom or finding their destiny (the continuous path through life that God assigned for you to walk). Satan uses negative circumstances and wrong people to keep you sidetracked. People influence people, and strong willed or charismatic personalities can be like unholy magnets, pulling Christian youth, who can be seduced by a person's looks, smiles, or charming personality, into their sphere of influence. Our desire for acceptance by peers can become the bait on the trap. We are often willing to compromise our commitment to Christ and personal convictions to gain that feeling of admiration that comes from being liked by others. Here is a question: If you were to be arrested for being a Christian, would there be enough evidence to convict you in court? Do your friends actually know you are a Christian or are you hiding your light in the darkness?

Always be aware that friends can quickly change. Jesus was received by multitudes, but when he was betrayed, the crowds turned against him while he stood before an illegal tribunal and fixed jury. The multitudes crying his praises, and shouting "Hosanna!" were missing, and his own disciples were fleeing like frightened pups running from a dog catcher. Public opinion of the Son of God changed so quickly that even his close friend, Peter, denied knowing Christ due to fear of punishment (Luke 22:33-34; 54-62). We must be careful in today's times, for these disciples were men who knew Him personally; the lesson must be learned that even his closest disciples denied Him through pressure.

WATCH OUT FOR TAR BABIES

Remember, unsaved individuals and lukewarm Christians can be very sly—like foxes. A fox is a very crafty creature in many ways, and can be tricky to catch. Because the fox is quite a curious creature, it can be caught with a tar baby. A farmer would take some straw and form it into a small man called a "straw baby." Then you apply black, sticky tar to the arms, legs, and body of the straw man - this is called a "tar baby." If a person takes their right hand to grab the object, that hand becomes stuck. The only way to escape is to take the left hand to help remove the other hand; that hand also becomes sticky and stuck by the tar. Then your only option is to take your left foot and try to pull your hands away; but soon, your foot is sticky with tar, and you are quickly in a mess with your entire body coated with tar, a very difficult substance to remove from the skin.

This story can be a metaphor for "sticky situations" you may encounter in your life, where all involvement (even in the solution to problems) causes a bigger issue.

Indeed, some people are so sticky and grimy (metaphorically speaking) that once you connect with them, pulling away is difficult and you become stuck in a mess. In life, you may have situations that become very frustrating, consuming your time and energy. Three times in my life, I have dealt with business individuals who did unethical things against our ministry, usually involving finances. Their actions were an aggravation that eventually turned into frustration, ending up in a tarred situation that I had to deal with. Eventually, I extracted myself and disconnected from them, as it was better for God Himself to deal with men like this than for me to do so.

It is interesting to note that this trap of the enemy has one easy solution: You must have friends and family, who with God's help and guidance pull you out of these sticky situations. Sometimes we let ourselves get "stuck" in our messes without communicating the problems and frustrations that they cause. In this tar scenario, a little force in the right direction could easily have broken the bonds of tar (the enemy). Don't allow the enemy to bind you with his chains and yokes.

TOO FAT FOR THAT

Chains and yokes represent the "weights and sins" that easily control a person (Heb. 12:1-2). If you were raised in a Spirit-filled church, you have probably heard the words "anointing" or "anointed" used to describe the tangible presence of God moving in the atmosphere, or the sensation of powerful, spiritual energy flowing through a person when worshipping or praying. The word "anoint" is found in both the Old and New Testaments. The practice of anointing originally began with ancient shepherds who would pour oil upon the heads of their sheep to prevent lice and flies from laying eggs on their heads or around the openings of their noses and ears. Once olive oil was rubbed onto the heads of the sheep, their wool was slippery, thus preventing insects from remaining on their wool. Rubbing oil on the sheep as such became a symbol of protection and blessing.

In the Old Testament, kings and priest were anointed with sacred oil. When this anointing ceremony was enacted, the Holy Spirit would then "come upon" the anointed person; thus, the pouring of oil was linked with the arrival of the Holy Spirit to anoint the person for a particular assignment. When David was a teenager, Samuel anointed him with oil, and the Spirit of the Lord came upon him. Soon thereafter, David boldly snuffed out the life of a giant named Goliath (see 1 Samuel 16 and 17).

In the New Testament, the Greek word for anoint is *chrio*, which means "to smear or rub with oil," which indicates being consecrated and set apart with the power of God for his purposes. The word "anointed" often refers to a person who has been chosen by God for a specific purpose; in Hebrew Christ is called the *Mashiach*, meaning the "anointed one." Thus, the anointing is an act, and the anointed person becomes set apart for God's purposes. The anointing is not a figment of the mind or imagination, as the anointing can be felt within and upon a person. One amazing manifestation of the Holy Spirit is that He can actually be *felt* when He is near, creating a tangible atmosphere when He hovers over people. This feeling of anointing blossoms into joy and peace, two positive emotions that can break the oppressive feelings of sin and bondages.

When it comes to any form of bondage, addiction, or sin lifestyle, it takes a *strong anointing* to break a stronghold in the mind or spirit of a person taken captive by Satan. I love the way Isaiah revealed this fact in Isaiah 10:27:

> "And it shall come to pass in that day, that his burden shall be taken away from off thy shoulder, and his yoke from off thy neck, and the yoke shall be destroyed because of the anointing."

Notice the yoke is something that binds a person or ties them to something else. Other translations note that this verse can read, *"The yoke shall be destroyed because of the fatness."* What does this mean? Figuratively, it can refer to an ox that has a wooden yoke connected to an ancient grinding handle around its neck, while going in circles, and grinding grain on a threshing floor. If the grain piled up and the ox continually ate, the neck of the ox would expand and eventually become too big for the yoke around its neck. Thus, the yoke is destroyed because of the "fatness!"

If a yoke is simply *broken*, it can be repaired; but if it is *destroyed*, it cannot be repaired and is no longer effective in binding the person as captive. The anointing of the Holy Spirit can and will destroy any Satanic bondage and stronghold to the point that it can't bind anymore. You will spiritually outgrow the very thing Satan is trying to use against you, leaving it in your past and walking away from it. Just as the ox continually eats, getting "too fat" for the yoke, your personal prayer life and feeding from the Word of God will enlarge your faith, and you will become "too fat for that," able to block what the enemy wants to hang around your neck.

Should you sense a need for destruction of a yoke, have anointed people pray over and agree with you that the yoke will be smashed, removing the mental chains and spiritual fetters connecting you to bondage. On several occasions, all it took was one strong encounter with God to bring a renewal to my mind and spirit. Once you are delivered, it will require personal *discipline* to remain free, which includes separating yourself from any hindrance that has held you back. Discipline is the self-control required to willfully refuse to return to the thing the Lord has delivered you from.

A vital spiritual discipline is reading the Word; the Bible is filled with practical life instructions and reading it provides needed insights that you can apply to your daily life. In addition, it is good to listen to the life experiences of other believers, both their successes and their failures, to glean important applications; they have been through similar experiences, and can help prevent pitfalls, roadblocks, and land mines that you too may encounter in this life.

In my early ministry as a teenage evangelist, I spent weeks on end studying the lives of the revivalists and evangelists from the 1940s who helped spearhead the Healing Restoration Revival. I read where some of these men with powerful ministries could not sleep at night, and were "advised" to drink some wine to help them sleep. Several became full-blown alcoholics, lost their families, ministries, and churches in some cases. I resolved never to touch alcohol in any form, as in the Bible drinking alcohol never led to anything good, only bad. This is an example of learning from other people's mistakes. Why repeat the same issues that cause others pain and grief? I also learned from their successes, how they reached multitudes, maintained global ministries, initiated partnerships, set up prayer meetings, and organized regional crusades. This proved to be a great assistance in building our own ministry outreaches and team organization, Voice of Evangelism. Learn from both the negative and positive experiences of others, and remember, the best lesson you will ever learn is to learn your lesson the first time.

Remember these four keys: enter a *redemptive covenant,* find your lifelong *occupation,* and find your *true love,* all while making the *right friends* along the way. These four major steps are keys to continual joy and happiness in life. At times you may make some bad choices, but repent and ask God for His direction. If you fall down spiritually, then get back up immediately. Remember, a failure does not need to be final and one bad moment does not need to ruin you for life. Trust in the Lord with all your heart and He will direct your paths (Prov. 3:5-6).

CHAPTER 3

DANGERS IN THE DATING GAME

H AVE YOU EVER wondered who makes up all of the dress fads and different catchwords that emerge in society? I remember phrases like "far out, man" from the 60's hippie movement. Then there was "cool, man," then "that's the bomb," and numerous others. Years ago, there were games that people in every home seemed to own, such as Monopoly, Scrabble, and Twister. From there, board games evolved into computer games and smart phone apps. Clothes continue to have their fad seasons, including colors and styles. Who starts all of these trends? It has a lot to do with the influence of television programs, movies, and celebrities. It is all just a clever bit of marketing. At times, some youth will feel "left out" if they are not wearing the latest brands or speaking the right phrases during a fad season. A similar burden emerges with the pressure to date as soon as possible.

During my many decades of ministry travels, the one area where more young people find themselves in an emotional trap is when falling into the dating game.

THE FROG MYTH

There is something I call *the Frog Myth*. There is a fairy tale (a type of folklore or short story, usually told to children) that involves a prince placed under some a curse requiring a beautiful princess to kiss him in order to turn him back into a prince. (Whoever wrote this story must have had a weird imagination because what girl in her right mind would kiss a slimy, ugly, croaking frog, especially in the mouth!) She ends up kissing the frog and instantly, the old, green, bumpy skin and bulging eyes are gone; before her stands this handsome, dreamy-eyed, perfect specimen of male anatomy. And like many other fairy tales, of course they live happily ever after.

I use this as a metaphor. At times I become astonished at dedicated, Christians girls who will attach themselves in a relationship to a *slimy* young man with no moral standards and little personal character. Often, he will be a deceiver and hang on to two girls at once in secret, jumping like a frog from one girl to the other, promising each girl she is the only one for him. Just like the story, some young girls date these frogs and believe that hanging out in the swamps and loving them will turn a toad into Prince Charming. This is why dating at a young age should be avoided. You end up giving a piece of your heart to every boy in your life until, at the end, you are the one with a broken heart. As a Christian, be patient and allow God to groom your soul mate.

BREAKING UP WITH THE DEVIL

When I was in High School, it was common for girls, especially cheerleaders, to hang out with the football players. If they were "dating" each other, she would proudly wear his high school jacket with the school letter sewn on the front. This act identified her as being linked with a certain player on the team, and it was an unspoken rule than none of the other players were to ask her out. Most of the time, the player himself was more than just a *football* player; he was *"playing* the field," checking out any other girl that might spike his interest. Once the fellow was exposed for his numerous secret rendezvous, the girl would break up with the unfaithful two-timer. She would give him back his ring and his jacket, and clear her locker of the pictures taped inside the door.

The devil is equally a liar and a deceiver and will whisper all kinds of worthless nonsense in your ears to gain access to your soul. Once you expose him, make a break from him and give him back his junk. Give him back the depression, suicidal thoughts, fear, anxiety, and let him know he is not welcome anymore.

THE REASON PEOPLE DATE

There is peer pressure to begin dating at age 16. This *terrible* idea is mostly influenced by the culture. In my teen years, I didn't have a youth pastor, or any mature youth leader in Dad's church to help direct me concerning this matter. My own father and mother never once had a discussion with me about the dangers of forming bonds with the opposite sex, or the stress involved if your emotions connect with another in your early teens. Back in that day, no one (at least that I knew) had conducted studies on the numerous chemicals that are released when two young people become physically attached to one another. And only recently have researchers learned how certain chemicals, released through kissing, actually bond two people together. One of the chemicals is dopamine, a "feel good" chemical linked to the reward center of the brain. This type of chemical is involved in the process of emotional bonding between two people. In one study, researchers blocked the dopamine receptors in small rodents and observed that when they did, the animals did not pair up together or mate. When the dopamine was later allowed release, the animals began pairing up, even if no actual mating occurred. I am certain God's true intent of these chemicals relates to attraction between a mature male and female, who would eventually marry and keep the emotion of love connecting them until parted in death.

Once physically or emotionally connected, breaking up with a person literally stops that chemical bond and can cause sudden depression, leading at times to suicidal thoughts. Certain "feel good" chemicals released during a relationship explain why often, when a boy breaks up with a girl, the girl is an emotional wreck for days; yet, the guy often moves immediately to another girl to satisfy his need to "feel good," since these chemicals are released on the brain through physical contact act like a drug! Once they cease, it creates the same feeling as an addict coming off of drugs and going "cold turkey." When a person is young and immature, they will "feel" they are in love when in reality they may be "in love" with the *feeling* and not necessarily in love with the person. This is clearly the case when, for example, a girl is abused verbally and physically, yet she continues to cling to her abuser like an addict needing a "fix." In extreme cases, separation, divorce, or broken relationships can put the body into crash mode while the mind spins in a whirlwind of confusion. This is going to sound really crazy to some youth, but ***avoid*** *one-on-one dating by your-selves, alone in an apartment or home, especially at an early age.* The enemy will attempt to use the opportunity to seize upon your weak moments, initiating things that can damage your future and impact a later marriage.

MY OWN NEGATIVE EXPERIENCES

I have discovered that one of the great lessons in life is to learn from the experiences of others, both their mistakes and successes, so you don't have to repeat the same bad patterns they experienced. You can spare yourself numerous heartaches by this method; in retrospect, I wish someone had imparted to me some *life advice* on this very subject in my earlier days. When I was a teen, the church instructed us to avoid anything that even *appeared* worldly; yet they seldom gave any reason or biblical evidence why to avoid certain "sins". I believe youth will do the right thing if they *know the reason*ing behind why not to do the wrong thing.

When I was 16 years of age, I "fell in love" (or what I thought was love) with a young girl in my dad's church. She could sing, play the piano, and was very dedicated to the Lord. I would talk to her as much as possible, and eventually became a bit jealous if any other young man gave her attention. I remember cutting grass and setting aside enough money to buy her a rather nice diamond engagement ring ($210.00). I requested to meet with her dad and told him I desired to marry her. With a blank stare on his face and monotone voice, he asked where I would work, and I replied, "The Kroger Grocery Store." I was still in high school and thought I had all of this figured out. He just continued staring at me and certainly did not place approval on this idea. Shortly thereafter, they moved to another state for her father's job. Once she was no longer near me, the "soul tie" was broken. It was at that same time I was called to ministry and began preaching in small churches in Virginia, West Virginia, and Maryland. In retrospect, I was immature at age 16, and far too young to even consider marriage, although I refused to listen to the wisdom of others reminding me of that fact. As kids mature, there is a natural feeling that develops towards the opposite sex. However, it is a fact that girls mature physically and emotionally faster than boys. We have a large number of single teenagers at our OCI ministry, and we try to instruct through what we've learned from our experiences — both the negative and the positive.

In the past, people would marry younger to begin their families, as most of life's activities and "jobs" centered on a family farm (at least in the South). This required a large number of children in each family to help work the fields and carry daily responsibilities. My Father, Fred Stone, was born to a family with 12 kids, some that passed away shortly after birth. Growing up, all of them lived in one log-cabin house and shared rooms and responsibilities. Today, most families have on average two or three children.

Years ago, from childhood through their teen years, young men were required to work on the farms without pay as part of their "chores," forcing them to mature earlier. Studies now indicate that young men are mentally and emotionally maturing much later in life. In fact, some doctors believe that this later maturity, which usually happens between 24 to 28 years of age, can be a result of young boys spending hours a day playing computer games and staying glued to social media, as the fantasy world of electronics has literally re-wired the neurons of the brain. While this is not the case with every young man, the delayed maturity syndrome appears to be widespread. I have seen young girls "crash and burn" after being led along the "path of love," only to be dumped for another girl whose presence "releases more chemicals" than the previous one. Love is more than a feeling or emotion, as true love is built on trust and mutual dreams and desires through the will of God. Look, having a small pet like a cat or dog can make you feel good, as does a chocolate milkshake or a huge chocolate chip cookie. Feelings will fluctuate, changing your opinions based upon circumstances, but real love remains, as those happily married can testify.

LISTEN TO WISE ADVICE

When you are mature enough to date, you should first have the approval of your parents or guardians. If you are a girl, the young man should talk directly to your parents or guardians and specific guidelines must be made clear up front. However, if at any time those who are responsible for your care and guardianship say they prefer you not go out with a certain person or even hang around them, do not throw a tantrum or get into an argument. Gently ask why they feel that way and be obedient, as at times parents (especially a mom) can pick up that the heart or motive of a person is not pure. Trust me, your life will not end and fall apart just because you didn't get to go to a movie with "Billy Bob" or "Suzie Q." Life will continue. It is never bad to "lose a friend that is not really a friend," and at times instead of closing your bedroom door and sulking in rejection, close your door and jump around the room saying, "Thank you Lord for watching out for me and replacing them with someone I need in my life."

THE TRIALS OF DATING AS A YOUNG MINISTER

At age 18 when I was beginning my evangelistic ministry, one of the first conversations I had that cautioned me as a traveling evangelist not to date "one on one" or alone was with one of my mentors, M.H. Kennedy. This man of God was state overseer of the Church of God in Virginia where I began conducting local church revivals. M.H. called me in his office and said, "I am going to talk to you like a father would his son." I then received a 20-minute lecture on the danger of some of the church girls that are not as "sanctified" (set apart for God) as I may think. He continued, saying that some of the young women have a mind set to marry a preacher; I must have discernment not to fall into a trap, as their motives for being my "friend" may not be sincere. He told me that dating or going out with any girl in a revival would cause problems leading to contention among the other youth, hindering the flow and taking a toll on any revival. He rather bluntly shared other things that I will omit.

He spoke to me shortly after I had already learned a very embarrassing lesson. I had become friends with some Christian girls at a youth camp. I was not "dating" any of them, but just hanging around them and other youth. Unknown to me, they were more "serious" about me than just a casual friendship. I was preaching a tent revival in Hillsville, Virginia, when out of the blue three girls showed up at the same service, all of them wanting to "go out and eat with me after church." It was a bit embarrassing and the pastor, who was my best friend and about my age, laughed and said, "That will teach you a lesson about being friendly to too many at once."

I did take M.H. Kennedy's advice. In those days, after evening services, young people would head to a restaurant or fast food chain to eat and "fellowship." I would drive to the place to sit with the youth group or with the pastor and his wife, talking with all of them and not just one person in particular. Although it was a normal thing for a single young man to talk to young women, I tried to be cautious, knowing that in the future I would marry a woman of God's choosing.

A DREAM LEADS TO GOD'S WILL

In my earlier days, I met a young woman who was a pastor's daughter and felt as though this would be the girl I would marry. We built a strong friendship over time, and after one year eventually became engaged. There were numerous people, especially close friends who were ministers, who began sensing in their spirits that she was not the perfect will of God for my life. I recall in November of that year (1979), receiving a phone call from my fellow evangelist friend, Marcus Lamb, who said, "Perry I was praying for you and you are not to marry the girl you are engaged to. It is not the will of God." After a while, other close friends were also sensing that this was not God's will. Through this I learned that at times, *people on the outside often have a clearer view than you do up close!* When numerous people you trust are telling you the *same thing,* and warning you that the relationship you are in is not the right one, you need to get a "Joseph" anointing: Flee from that relationship as Joseph did when he ran out of the house from Potiphar's wife (see Genesis 39).

In November of that same year (1979), I experienced a vision that eventually realigned me into God's perfect plan. I was in Danville, Virginia, in the West Main Church of God basement, lying on my back with my Bible under my head. Suddenly, I saw a full-color vision of M.H. Kennedy, who was then the state overseer of the Church of God offices in Alabama, standing behind his office desk. At that time, I was scheduled to preach in Birmingham, Alabama, in February; in this vision M.H. said, "Perry, do not go to the church in Birmingham to preach that revival. They are having problems. God has another door." I jumped up off the floor, amazed. In obedience to the vision, I called the pastor from Birmingham that night and told him I felt I should cancel the February meeting. I was amazed when the pastor replied that he may be leaving and taking another church, as there were problems at the Birmingham church (which is what Kennedy had said in the vision). That following week, I received a letter from Joe Edwards, the Evangelism director for the Church of God in Alabama at the time, that a door was opened for me to conduct a revival at the Northport Church of God in Northport, Alabama. I knew nothing about this church, but replied that I would go the first week of February—replacing the same week that I had canceled services with the Birmingham pastor.

Late-December a few weeks later, I experienced a detailed dream of a church I had never seen. In the dream I was walking out of a men's restroom, and on the right was a water fountain. In front of me was a wooden door with a small glass frame allowing me to see the sanctuary, shaped like a large square with four sections of orange pews and matching orange carpet. The youth were situated on the far end and people were walking to the choir loft to sing. I heard the Lord tell me, *"You will have the greatest revival in the history of this church!"* Then I awoke, not knowing where this church was; I was certain I had received a spiritual dream.

In January 1980, I was conducting revivals in Kimberly and Selma, Alabama. One morning, I related this strange dream of the church I saw to Mark Jacobs, pastor of the Selma church. Mark replied, "That sounds like the church they built in Northport—my home church." I felt a chill go down my spine. He said, "Let's drive to Northport so you can see if it is the same building." When I arrived at Northport, the pastor, Walter Mauldin, met us at the door. Standing in the small church lobby, I told him my dream. He was amazed, then showed me the exact locations of the men's room, water fountain, side door, and the orange pews and carpet. It was the exact building I'd seen in the dream! I said to him, "The Lord told me we would have the greatest revival in the history of this church!"

GOD HAD A BIGGER PLAN

God orchestrated this revival using a vision and a dream because His purpose went beyond soul-winning. It was during the second week of the Northport revival that I received an unexpected phone call from the girl I was engaged to in Virginia, and we agreed that we should break off any wedding plans. It is always difficult to sever any relationship that you have built, especially one which involves daily conversations over time. At first, it felt like a death. If you experience a broken relationship, you must keep saying to yourself, "God has something better. God is orchestrating my life. I am moving into God's will." As difficult as it may be, don't become despondent and depressed because the person broke up with you. God may be moving you from something good to something greater—His best!

It was during the third week of this Northport revival that a moment of divine revelation struck, changing the course of my life. It was February 1980, and the church choir was singing when the time for prayer requests arrived. As the congregation joined in prayer, I turned to my left, observing about 70 youth standing and praying in one section. Half way back, standing near the aisle, was a beautiful young lady. I recall she was wearing a black skirt and black jacket, a white blouse with elegant sleeves and a high, frilly collar. She had beautiful, long brunette hair that was curled at the end. She had her eyes closed and her hands held high praying. She looked like a human angel. I suddenly heard these words: "That is the girl you are going to marry!" I knew the voice of the Holy Spirit but at the same time I stood stunned. I thought perhaps the enemy was attempting to distract my mind with this very attractive young woman. I began rebuking the thought by saying under my breath, "I rebuke this in Jesus name!" After saying this, I immediately heard the same words repeated again: "You will marry this girl." At that moment, this word dropped from my head into my spirit. I knew without a doubt that this was the girl the Lord had prepared for me to be with.

When the revival concluded, I began to call the Skelton family (the church family she was staying with), and Pam would usually answer the phone. We would chat briefly. This led to me writing her (this was before texting or social media). She was so cute and her southern accent made me swoon. She was gentle-spirited and also a great cook. It took me about three months before I told her what occurred that night and the word of the Lord that I would marry her. Before telling her, I asked her what feelings she had about me. I learned she had told her closest friend, "I love him, I really do."

It was several years later on April 2, 1982, that I walked Pamela Taylor, adorned in a flowing white dress, down the aisle of the Northport Church of God and vowed my life to her. Since 1982, my little "Pammy Poo," or "Poohster," or "Pooh Bear" (she has many nicknames) has been my greatest fan, helper, confidant, and friend. She has stood faithfully with me through good and bad, trials and blessings, and she is my soul mate.

THE LORD'S CHOICE

Why did the Lord look down in Northport, Alabama, and choose Pam to be my wife? The answer is because she perfectly fits numerous needs I would have in ministry. From a natural perspective, she has said, "I would consider myself the last girl on the list to be married to Perry Stone." First, she was from a divorced family and not parented in a strong Christian home. Second, as teenagers, she and her sisters were displaced and moved in with a church family, who took them into their own home after her mother experienced a complete nervous breakdown. Third, her father was absent from her life as a teenager, which can sometimes cause "abandonment issues" in girls; yet thankfully, this never affected her. Finally, Pam's only main "job" before we were married was working as a babysitter for a family with several young children, making $50.00 a week.

How could a young girl with that type of résumé and background, lacking "secular work experience," marry a minister and travel across the nation, work as the secretary and continually manage the numerous duties of a ministry that would eventually be internationally known? Wouldn't she need a business degree to assist in overseeing a multi-million-dollar ministry? Shouldn't she have experienced abandonment issues, low self-esteem, and daily regrets, wishing things in her family would have turned out better? Shouldn't she worry about a possible "generational curse" from the divorce or her mother's breakdown, thinking perhaps this spirit would also attack her? The answer is "No!" If you ask her how she has moved forward in such a positive manner in her life, she would tell you her "secret" has been choosing not to allow anything from her past to impact her future. Pam is stable, mature, caring, and loving; She is a person who does not look back when she is moving forward.

One of the greatest advantages of her circumstances was the

fact that she did not feel the pressure that younger wives do, to go home to her mom and dad every month or so for a visit. For many years (before her mother passed away), Pam did bring her mom, Stella, up to Cleveland each spring, and she usually enjoys visiting her two sisters and their children twice a year in Alabama. Pam was totally connected to me from the beginning. I recall once spending 16 weeks on the road in revivals (that's 112 consecutive days), and not one time did she ever complain and ask to "go home."

Pam is a great example that you *cannot judge a person's future based on circumstances in their past.* Nothing and no one except God Himself prepared her for her future in ministry. God knew Pam's heart and saw a teachable spirit and a vessel He could mold for His purposes. There were gifts within her that emerged over time. She has an amazing talent to cook, is gifted at hospitality, and is a homemaker and powerful teacher to our two children. Most of all, she is an example of what a minister's wife should be.

FOR THOSE WITH CHRISTIAN PARENTS

If you have Christian parents, or someone like a guardian that is sincerely watching out for your soul and best interests, pay attention to their instructions, even when it is not what you want to hear. A parent who loves their child will be protective of that child, no matter what age they are. When you don't come home on time, they are calling because worrying thoughts that you may be in harm's way flash through their minds. You may know everything around you is ok at that moment, but parents are not mind readers. When you are an hour late at curfew, they worry. They desire to train you up in the understanding and principles of the Lord, as it is written, "Train up a child in the way they should go; and when he is old he shall not depart from it" (Proverbs 22:6).

Years ago, my son was struggling with some unhealthy habits and his mom was up late, trying to reach him with no response. When he came home, she said to him, "You won't understand why I'm so concerned about you until you have children of your own!" Proverbs teaches, *The rod of reproof gives wisdom but a child left to himself brings his mother shame" (Prov. 29:15).* Respect your Christian parents the way you would want to be respected if you were a parent, because one day you may be!

READ PROVERBS TO RECEIVE WISDOM

One of the world's most respected and noted evangelists said that he reads the book of Proverbs every day. Proverbs was mainly written by Solomon (and a few other writers), and is considered by scholars to be "wisdom literature." Three key words are found in Proverbs: knowledge, understanding, and wisdom. Knowledge is when you *accumulate* information and facts; understanding is properly *arranging* that information and knowledge in a correct order; and wisdom is the ability to *apply* what you have learned in a practical manner. I suggest you read on a continual basis the 31 chapters penned in the book of Proverbs, as the advice given in these verses includes wise sayings and life instructions from Solomon, a man considered to be one of the wisest who ever lived.

Here is one example. In Proverbs 23:29-33, the wise man begins revealing the danger of drinking wine. It reads:

"Who has woe? Who has sorrow? Who has contentions? Who has complaints? Who has wounds without cause? Who has redness of eyes? Those who linger long at the wine, those who go in search of mixed wine. Do not look on the wine when it is red, when it sparkles in the cup, when it swirls around smoothly; at the last it bites like a serpent, and stings like a viper. Your eyes will see strange things, and your heart will utter perverse things."

Let me make an important observation about alcohol. I have observed ministers who were raised knowing that drinking any form of alcoholic beverages opens doors to other forms of vices. It has been my observation for over 40 years that when ministers of the Gospel begin to drink, their inhibitions are soon removed, and often their clothes come off when their inhibitions depart. A close friend of mine that was once a heavy drinker, now saved, told me that he would always go to the bar, try to find the prettiest girl, and buy her drinks until she was drunk, afterward taking "advantage" of her as the next morning she couldn't remember what they did.

Another wise warning in Proverbs 1:10-16 reads:

"My son, if sinners entice you, do not consent. If they say, 'Come with us, let us lie in wait to shed blood; let us lurk secretly for the innocent without cause; let us swallow them alive like Sheol and whole, like those who go down to the pit; we shall find all kinds of precious possessions, we shall fill our houses with spoil; cast in your lot among us, let us all have one purse.' My son, do not walk in the way with them,

keep your foot from their path; for their feet run to evil, and
they make haste to shed blood."

Bad people will help you make bad decisions, but good people
will direct you to good choices. You can make a big mistake by
allowing a person who always pulls you into trouble stay in your
life longer than they should. Some things and some people just
need to be let go. Never ruin a good day by always thinking about
a bad day from the past. Just release the bad days and bad people
from the past so as not to ruin your present. I have spent time
trying to help people who really just wanted attention, not my
spiritual advice or help. It was like watering dead plants. Nothing
you do can make them grow and produce fruit. Surround yourself
with as many strong, believing friends as possible and only take
advice from the Bible, good parents, friends who are believers, and
friends who believe in you.

THE DANGER OF REBELLION

Proverbs 14:12 reads, *"There is a way that seems right to a person but
the end thereof are the ways of death."* Proverbs 16:18 explains, *"Pride
goes before destruction and a haughty spirit before a fall."* Rebellion
is a refusal to obey instruction or rules. Proverbs 17:11 says, *"An
evil man seeks only rebellion, therefore a cruel messenger will be sent
to him."* Often, the feeling of rejection is the root cause of rebellion. Rejection implies to refuse something, or to throw it away
as having no value. When parent's divorce, their children often
become attacked by a spirit of rejection which causes them to
feel insecure, leading to verbal abuse of the parents, and rebellion

against any form of authority. At times, a child will discover they were originally an unwanted conception. The mother may have attempted an abortion, or the mother was dissatisfied with something regarding the child. Each person reading this should realize that you are not a biological accident, or an afterthought of a one-night stand. Just as Jeremiah, God knew you before you were born (Jer. 1:5), and like David, He has created you specifically (Psa. 139:14-16). He also knew your name before your conception (see Luke 1:13).

Christ himself was "despised and rejected of men," and was "a man of sorrow and familiar with grief." Isaiah also said he was "despised," a Hebrew word meaning to disdain or to scorn (Isa. 53:3). People often picture Jesus as a tall, suntanned Nazarene, who was stunningly handsome and physically attractive. However, Isaiah 53 (which is a lengthy prophecy about Jesus the Messiah) tells us, "There is no beauty in him that we should desire" (Isa 53:2). Christ's gifting was not his appearance, but His anointing!

Often a person can become so "rejection oriented" that they perceive everything as rejection. Just because a person may disagree with your opinion is not a sign of personal rejection. An opinion is just that—an opinion—and is not immediately a sign of an attack on you, your statement, or idea. A person's body language can falsely make you believe you are being rejected, such as when you are talking and they are interrupting. This can be a person's personality trait, as some people have a bit of attention deficiency. At times I will interrupt a person, not to be rude, but if I don't say what I am thinking, I may forget what I was going to say (it gets that way as you get older)! At times I will simply ask, "Did you hear what I said," or "Were you paying attention," to prevent me from walking off feeling hurt, as I know what it is to battle rejection and I will attempt to cut it off at the seed before it can take root.

Recall the statement in this section's opening paragraph: Rejection may become the root cause leading to rebellion. Remember that rebellion is so serious that God places it in the same category as witchcraft (see 1 Sam. 15:23). Manipulation is linked to witchcraft, and those in rebellion often rebel to see a certain *response* from the person they are rebelling against. Those who consistently rebel, at times enjoy watching others' *reaction* to their actions, hoping the person they are targeting will feel hurt on the same level they are hurting. However, Proverbs warns that a "cruel messenger," or an evil spirit, would be released upon those in rebellion. King Saul's sin was pride and rebellion: His jealousy toward David opened a door for an evil spirit that continually tormented Saul (see 1 Sam. 16:14-16; 16:23; 18:10).

As a youth, you should pray every day for wisdom. James said if you lack wisdom then you should ask God, who will liberally impart it to you (see James 1:5). Wisdom is the quality of having good judgment when making decisions. Dating the right person requires making a good decision, and choosing your soul mate for marriage must be decided in wisdom. True wisdom can discern the proper time and manner in which to act upon or react to something or someone. Pray for wisdom and if you have a "check" in your spirit, then let go and let God take it from there. As a wise person said, "Giving up does not always mean that you are weak but sometimes indicates that you are strong enough to let go."

I went through a very brief period of rebellion in my mid-teens. Thankfully, it was short lived and an all-night prayer meeting knocked that old rebellious spirit when the Lord imparted to me a gentler and more mellow heart. In retrospect, I believe my rebellion opened a door to an evil spirit that troubled my mind for several months; when I released the individuals that were the root of my rebellion, I received freedom in my mind and spirit. Sometimes the Lord will remove certain people from you, and you then become upset and angry. Nevertheless, you will look back years later and realize the Lord was actually protecting and watching out for you, keeping you from making a wrong decision and ruining your potential.

CHAPTER 4

WHEN THE ENEMY DISCERNS DIVINE MOMENTS

O N JUNE 23, 1959, I was born in a small rural hospital in Parsons, West Virginia, to a young minister and his wife, Fred and Juanita Stone. Mom told me that after birth, I was unable to hold down any breast milk from my mother or even formula. The doctor kept me for several weeks for tests and finally said I needed soy milk. Mom said I threw up that milk and it caused my clothes to smell. They are not sure why my stomach was so sensitive, but I managed to survive and make it until I was old enough for other sustenance.

I don't remember much of my first five years except, for some reason, I can recall the moments before a terrifying car accident. Dad, Mom, and I were in the front seat of a white 1961 Comet, headed to Elkins, West Virginia, with two young men they knew riding in the back seat. As the story is told, Dad topped the hill of a two-lane road, when he saw in front of him a truck—without brake lights—sitting in Dad's lane. He was going to pass the truck when another large pick-up truck traveling at high speed suddenly appeared in the other lane, leaving only one option: to slam on the brakes and hit the truck at 55 miles per hour. In those days, there were no seat belts; thus, the impact sent my mother's head into the windshield, breaking her jaw and crushing her right knee. My dad was gripping the steering wheel; upon impact, his hands bent the steering wheel across the steering column, injuring his larynx and voice box. From 1961 until his death at age 78, this accident caused Dad to speak with a rasp. The two young men riding in the back received minor injuries when upon impact their hands pierced the white back seat covers, thrusting them into the springs of the car seats.

I had been standing up in the front seat between Mom and Dad when, moments before impact, Dad said to Mom, "Make him sit down. If we had an accident, he would go through the windshield!" Minutes later when dad smashed into the back of the truck, I was thrown into the dashboard. When Mom regained her composure a bit, she saw my limp body lying in glass on the floor. I wasn't moving, and her mind raced with the fearful thought that I had broken my neck in the impact. In pain, she prayed that God not let me die, at which point I gasped for air and began crying out saying, "My shoe, my shoe!" (The impact had forced a shoe from my foot.) Some church members drove to the crash site to take me, while Mom and Dad were rushed to the hospital.

Nearly 40 year later, before my dad went to Heaven, we were discussing the 1961 accident and how one or all of us could have been killed. Dad reflected: "Son, years ago I used to think the enemy was using that accident to try to kill me, as I was starting a church in that area and the accident created a huge delay and hindrance. However, as years passed I have realized that you were the target. The enemy wanted you dead as a child to stop your future ministry that would reach millions of people." Dad had reached thousands but his son has reached millions. God protected us both from a premature death on a country road outside of Elkins, West Virginia, ensuring we would fulfill His end-time destiny.

Here is a *secret* that Satan doesn't want you to know. Jesus Christ has stripped Satan from his key (authority) over death (see Rev. 1:18). While all men are appointed once to die (Heb. 9:27), it is Christ, not Satan, that controls the timing of your departure. If Satan had authority over death, he would have removed anointed ministers before they ever began their ministries!

Solomon, however, wrote that a person should not die before their time (Eccl. 7:17). Dying before your appointed time is called a "premature death." An early departure can be a result of a dangerous habit that you never gain control over (such as smoking, drug addiction, or alcohol abuse) or not caring for your physical body. Our bodies are the temple of the Holy Spirit, which we must protect.

THEN AND NOW

I often ask myself, "What will the America of the future look like when my children's children are grown?" When I was a five-year-old little lad, we lived in Big Stone Gap, a small, rural town in the mountains of Southwestern Virginia. During the warm summers, there was no air conditioning in our small house, and each bedroom had windows we opened to remained cool. Luckily, these windows had built-in screens that helped restrain flies from food in your kitchen and tiny mosquitoes from making your arm a landing strip for a midnight snack.

I remember late at night hearing crickets chirp so loud that it sounded like tryouts for a mass insect choir. Near the ponds, the deep croaking of frogs having conversations with their friends broke through the night air, often keeping me awake and at other times, like an uninterpretable lullaby, boring me to sleep. In retrospect, any person with an evil intent living in the community could have popped out the screen and easily crawled into the window to snatch me or one of my siblings out of the bedroom. However, times were different then, and even sinners maintained certain moral values.

The school I attended was located only half a mile from home. I can recall my first day of school, walking to class by crossing a concrete bridge, passing by the local jail near a small bakery, crossing a road and trudging up the hill beside the Assembly of God Church, then topping the hill bordering the school's property. I remember one day turning back on the bridge and running back home crying. Mother met me at the door saying, "What's wrong?" In tears I replied, "Mommy, I don't want to go to school and leave you because I will forget what you look like." We walked to and from school in the heat, cold, rain, and sunshine. Today, no parent would allow their five-, six-, or seven-year-old to walk to school and back alone, simply for fear of them being abducted by some perverted person.

Sunday church services were always a bit different. My dad's church had about 60 members, and for the seven years he pastored there, the same four men and women served as our "special singers," essentially singing the same songs week after week, month after month, and year after year. There was no such thing as "praise and worship;" we simply sang music from a red-back hymnal or "mountain songs" written by common people. Services were very routine and predictable, but the people were sweet, hardworking, and steadfastly praying folks. The "breaks" we experienced from this normal structure were occasional revivals, when traveling evangelists or tent preachers erected their small tents in an open field near the church. Revivals in the church felt like a pause in the regular routine. These services were marked with preaching and the gifts of the Spirit were commonly manifested. During these services, the Holy Spirit would operate in various ways. The first time I ever saw a demonic manifestation was about age five in the church where Dad pastored, when a young man writhed like a serpent on the floor. Dad, along with several elders, cast an evil spirit out from him. I saw something odd that I recall to this day: The moment he was set free, a strange looking form came out of his mouth. It was about 12 inches long and almost looked like a transparent bubble. I believe, for some reason, I visibly saw some type of demonic spirit.

Each church in the denomination had a youth emphasis called

YPE or Young People's Endeavor. (I can tell some older folks came up with that name!) Once a month, the youth of the district joined together at one of the local churches, packing out the small, white-framed or brick churches with youth singing and adult preaching. After service, in the basement downstairs, we would devour hot dogs smothered with homemade chili and onions. We left full both spiritually and physically, speaking in tongues with onion breath!

THE BAPTISM THAT CHANGED MY LIFE

At age eleven, I attended a Church of God youth camp on the Roanoke, Virginia campground. On a hot, humid Thursday night in June, under an open-air, metal tabernacle, that I knelt on a concrete floor at a long, wooden altar bench, asking God to baptize me in the Holy Spirit. At first, my prayer was a bit slow and repetitious but as time passed, I entered a "zone" or spiritual dimension that was unknown to me before. I now call this "The Throne Zone." That night I discovered what I had heard older folks often testify about—that God's Presence could be "felt." My normal eleven-year-old, short and sweet, bow-my-head then go-my-way prayer was stretched into an hour-long, weeping encounter with the Divine, that concluded with me receiving the Baptism of the Holy Spirit and speaking a new tongue. I was so full of God's anointing that I was "drunk in the Holy Spirit," meaning I could barely stand up, and before I knew it, was being helped to my dorm room. I felt as though I were stuck somewhere between heaven and earth—needing to come back to earth and sleep but preferring to go up a little higher in God's Spirit. A friend and I literally stumbled back to the dorm room while speaking in a strange language, leaning on each other to prevent falling to the ground.

In retrospect, this one night and single encounter with God as a kid was a distinct mark that would initiate my future destiny as a minister. During many years of ministry, I have seen over 140 thousand persons receive the Holy Spirit baptism with the evidence of speaking in other tongues. This unique experience, called "praying in the Holy Ghost," moves you into a deeper relationship with God and a deeper level in prayer, enabling you to pray the will of God in every situation (see Romans 8:26-28).

Although my dad was the pastor of the church, I was too shy to tell him or Mom about my experience in receiving the Spirit. It would be weeks later that one of our church members, who served as a counselor at the camp and had prayed with me that night, informed my mom of what had occurred. For some reason, I did not speak in tongues again until I was about 16, during an extended revival. This was not because I had "lost the Holy Spirit," but as the Scripture indicates, you must "stir up the gift that is within you" (2 Tim. 1:6). I was still young, spending time hanging around friends, playing, goofing off; though still a strong believer, the fire had died out and I was like any average church kid. When I was 16, I discovered the Holy Spirit and fire, the phrase mentioned in Matthew 3:11.

The Holy Spirit baptism brings a "fire." On the Day of Pentecost, the Holy Spirit came into the upper room as "tongues of fire" (Acts 2:1-4). When you are totally filled with the Spirit, an invisible fire begins to burn in your spirit. Fire can burn out the impurities in precious metals such as silver and gold. In the same way, the

Spirit's fire helps remove impurities in your life. Fire also brings light, just as the Spirit of God illuminates your mind with the Word. Fire causes warmth, and with the Holy Spirit fire follows purification, illumination, and inspiration. The fire of the Spirit is also a metaphor for the zeal of the Lord: The Greek word for "zeal" is *zelos* and means to be "boiling hot, or to be fervent." Your zeal reveals where your passion is. It is zeal that stirs a desire to be in God's House, to attend a revival or conference, to worship and to pray. We are told to not be *"slothful in business but fervent in spirit serving the Lord,"* (Rom. 12:11).

How do you "stay on fire" for God? One key is to *never replace your first love with another love.* John told the church at Ephesus they had "left their first love" (Rev. 2:4). Have you observed when you focus on the Lord and His Word, your spirit always desires to be in His presence? However, when cares of life, love for riches, and lust of other things enter, they "choke God's Word" (see Matt. 13:18-22). When you love someone, you love talking to them, being with them, sharing time in their presence. Love for Christ is similar to this. The more quality time you spend with the Lord, the more this desire increases.

Romans 12:11 indicates we maintain zeal by "serving the Lord." In all my years of ministry, the most "fired up" believers are those who are always looking for something they can do for the Kingdom of God. It is interesting that one of the Greek words used for "serving" in the Bible literally means "kicking up dust" or "being on the move." Those who are true servants of Christ cannot sit still as they are always in motion. Being busy for busyness' sake is not ministry, but being busy and desiring to work, when there is a need, is required for a true servant of God.

Just as iron can sharpen iron, being near people on fire will spark a fire in your spirit. When I want to get inspired to pray, I get near intercessors. Whebusynessn I want to get deep in the Word, I sit with ministers of the Gospel who love to preach. When Moses transferred the Spirit to seventy elders, two young men named Eldad and Medad were nearby and the anointing fell upon them both, even though they were not a part of the seventy. Just being close to the anointing caused a "rub off" effect and the same is true with me and you. When we come near the presence of God in someone's life, if we are receptive, the presence of God will rub off on us!

BATTLES COME BEFORE BREAKTHROUGHS

We often hear ministers speak of receiving a "breakthrough." During the reign of David, the Philistines were attempting to encircle Jerusalem. God instructed David to attack them and he did, winning a great victory at a place called *Baal-perazim*, a name meaning "master or Lord of the breakthrough." David compared his war victory to water breaking out of an enclosed area. In today's vernacular, doctors will say that they have found a "breakthrough cure" for a certain disease. A breakthrough is an answer to a situation that was being hindered or seemed impossible. You can pray for one thing for years and suddenly the answer comes. We often say, "We received our prayer breakthrough." Perhaps a person needed additional finances or they were losing their home, when an unexpected check came in the mail, bringing a "financial breakthrough." Or maybe someone was praying for a family member for years and suddenly they repent and are saved. This is a breakthrough.

Remember that often, prior to a major breakthrough, there will be an increase in intense warfare. Before Joseph was exalted to second in command in Egypt, he was imprisoned for many years. Before David was crowned king of Israel, he experienced Ziklag where he lost everything and needed to pursue his enemies to recover it all, including the families of his 600 men of war (see 1 Sam 30). Moses spent 40 years on the back side of a desert watching sheep, prior to becoming pastor of an estimated 2 million-member church in the wilderness for roughly 40 years. Christ was tempted by the devil 40 days in the wilderness before beginning his 42 months of miraculous public ministry (Luke 4:2).

When I began my traveling ministry at age 18, I studied, prayed, and fasted continually. For a six-month period I tapped into the spirit world, and literally heard and saw demonic spirits appearing in hotel rooms and in homes where I stayed while ministering at churches. I am certain this was to frighten and intimidate me, and for a season of several months it was rather tormenting. However, on January 1, 1979, I received a breakthrough when I heard the Lord speaking into my right ear, saying, "As long as you live Satan will use what you see, feel, and hear against you. It is time to stand on the one thing that can never be moved. Stand on my Word." From that moment, the sounds, voices, and apparitions ceased, and I began spending no less than eight hours every day studying the Word of God or reading books related to spiritual and theological subjects.

When you are engaged in a battle, it often does not lift until you have learned the lesson God desires us to learn from the conflict. When in a spiritual battle, remember: They do not last forever, you will learn a valuable truth or lesson from it, and there is always a breakthrough of some form on the other side. The enemy does discern divine moments and divine movement at times, but he will never have the final word on the outcome. God controls that!

CHAPTER 5

GOD MADE THE DEVIL PAY

L OOKING BACK OVER the past few years I am very humbled and amazed at what the Lord has done. Our services at OCI (Omega Center International) have seen tens of thousands of youth attend numerous youth gatherings, and to receive salvation and the Holy Spirit baptism. The Omega Ranch, where the OCI property and buildings reside, was birthed out of great prayer and near-tragedy.

Years ago, unknown to my wife and I, my only son, Jonathan, was struggling with an addiction to a certain type of drug. We were unaware of the danger he had placed himself in. While at home one night, my wife, Pam, said she was burdened for our two children and wanted to pray. Our daughter Amanda ran into the living room and we called our son downstairs. He was sweating and seemed to be very jumpy and a bit agitated. A few moments later we were rushing to the emergency room after he admitted to taking a massive quantity of pills. He was not attempting suicide but had become addicted to the effects of a substance found in a certain type of drug. The ER heart monitor showed his heart was beating a dangerous 195 beats per minute.

Unknown to him, the doctor called me aside and said, "We have had 18 kids in this town die of overdoses this year..." Suddenly I felt my heart sink. I realized 18 parents had stood where I was standing—not knowing they would never take their child home with them again. I began praying in the Holy Spirit in my prayer language, and *rebuking the spirit of death* from my only son. At that time, I really didn't care who saw me or heard me, or about anyone's opinion. I felt I was standing in the gap between possible life and death.

Standing in the ER beside my son, who was hooked up to various monitors, something happened that would forever change my life and my future. As my son lay there on that bed, the doctor handed him a small device and said, "If you have a sudden chest pain, hit this button immediately." He placed a small object with a button on top in his left hand. As he walked out, he turned, and in a somber tone said, "But, if that happens and your heart stops, I can't guarantee that I can bring you back."

At that moment two things happened. First was a fear that struck both me and my son. I could see it in his face. This was no longer a "good feeling from getting high," or "a time to escape reality, then come back." This was literally life or death. The thought entered my head, "Could my son's life actually be taken from him as a teenager?" He never saw this coming, and neither did 18 other youth, who were "just having fun" at the homes of others experimenting with drugs, then rushed to the ER.

I will never forget the look in my son's eyes when he said, "Dad you have to pray for me. Pray I won't die." I felt a burden hit me that I cannot explain. It would take God alone to intervene. I began to pray and speak life, rebuking the assignment of the enemy. I watched the heart monitor for two hours, knowing this was the most critical time.

Early in the morning, I followed a few medical staff and the gurney my son was laying on to a private room. He had been through a physical battle, and I a spiritual one. I was exhausted, mentally worn out, but now I was as angry as I had ever been. Not at him, but angry that the devil and his agents had taken the lives of 18 of teenagers in our area that year, under the watch of 380 churches in our county. Someone let them slip by. Where were the intercessors on those nights?

That's when I made a decree before God and to Satan: I said, "Satan, you will pay for what you did to my son and those other kids. In the name of the Lord I will do something to reach this generation and you will pay!" I never knew, until now, what that decree actually meant. In that dimly lit hospital room in the wee hours of the morning before sunrise, God heard what I said and chose to set a new assignment in motion. It would involve spiritually fathering a younger generation, and building a gathering place for them to meet and encounter a Word and visitation from God.

THE POWER OF KINGDOM CONNECTIONS

My friend Jentezen Franklin has a weekly telecast called *Kingdom Connections*. Christ is in charge of a Kingdom where He is the King and we are both his servants and ambassadors. Matthew's Gospel mentions the "parables of the Kingdom," and the Kingdom of heaven is a theme taught by Christ and John the Baptist. In this spiritual Kingdom, God connects individuals with one another for the purpose of advancing His Kingdom. Christ taught that when we give finances into His Kingdom, "men would give unto our bosom" (Luke 6:38); or stated another way, God would use other people to assist in providing the material and financial things. These acts of giving supply what we need to live and operate on the Earth and be successful citizens in a spiritual Kingdom whose authority can influence and even alter events on Earth.

This "Kingdom Connection Principle" activated God's formation of the OCI ministry. Years ago, Karen Wheaton, a noted youth leader in the Kingdom and founder of The Ramp in Hamilton, Alabama, came to Cleveland, Tennessee to organize The Ramp Cleveland, beginning with a handful of youth that grew into several hundred young people who gathered at Pathway Book Store on Thursday nights. Due to a series of circumstances, Karen turned the ministry over to another youth leader, who continued the weekly meetings and organized a prayer movement that continued successfully for some time. Eventually, the leader moved away, as the attendees of The Ramp Cleveland merged into other ministries in town.

At this time, Mark Casto was the personal assistant to Dr. T.L. Lowery, a general in the Kingdom, whose Global Foundation headquarters was also located in Cleveland, Tennessee. Mark went to Dr. Lowery and asked if he could start a Tuesday night service at the Global Center called The Extreme. Thus, on Tuesday nights, youth would gather for music and ministry. There were about twelve or so key young people in the group that were consistently involved and part of a leadership team.

One afternoon, while researching a message in my upstairs office at the Voice of Evangelism headquarters, I stopped typing on my laptop, leaned back in my chair, and asked God a simple question. I said, "If you tarry your coming and I have another twenty years remaining in ministry, what would you have me do?" I was totally unprepared for what occurred next. Instantly I heard these words in my spirit, "Do you want to go where I am going?" A bit stunned, I immediately replied, "Yes I do!" Then the Holy Spirit said, "I am going to the sons and daughters!" I knew He was referring to the Joel 2 prophecy that the "sons and daughters would prophesy" in the last days. I then heard words that would set me on a new and exciting assignment. The Spirit of God revealed, "I want you to father a generation." Without hesitation, I knew the meaning of this statement. In Malachi 4:5-6, the prophet spoke of "Elijah the prophet" and how "before the great and terrible day of the Lord," God would, "turn the hearts of fathers to the children and turn the hearts of the children to their fathers." This prophecy indicated that spiritual fathers would be required in the last days to lead the sons and daughters, as God would supernaturally connect them together.

I was uncertain how to do this "fathering thing," since most of my messages and outreaches in the VOE ministry were reaching an older generation mature in the Word, and my messages tended to be more prophetic in nature than geared toward a younger generation. The Lord impressed upon me to meet with Mark Casto, whom I had met briefly but never for any long conversation. I followed through with this word and went early to his service being conducted at the T.L. Lowery facility. I went to the small back room where Mark and several others were praying, and when the prayer ended, I asked to speak privately with him. I told him the word of the Lord, and how I would make myself available to assist in any possible way, including mentoring the youth in the ministry. To my amazement, he and several attending confirmed that Mark had felt impressed to pray for me, that my heart would turn toward this generation and I would be a spiritual father, especially for The Extreme (his Tuesday night service at the time). This began a connection (remember Kingdom Connections) and a spiritual bond that helped initiate what would become the future OCI ministry.

I began speaking occasionally at The Extreme. The Lord began dealing with me to rent a small facility in town to accommodate the Tuesday service. I rented a church with two rooms: the main sanctuary seated no more than 150 people. Services were moved to the facility and I hired a secretary to assist in the various responsibilities of a growing congregation. Using television and social media, I began announcing the Tuesday night gatherings. Mark preached the majority of the time, and I would only preach every four weeks or so. One of my strong gifts is administration and organization, and I began using these gifts to advance the ministry in every way possible. Eventually, we announced special events, first called Confluence, and later, Reformation; weekends where youth and adults gathered for powerful ministry. The attendance was small at first (80 or so people) but eventually grew to hundreds, with some families moving to Cleveland to be a part of the ministry.

The growth at the little facility demanded that I either find a larger building or build one. I began searching for land, and through some "God circumstances" was able to purchase over 78 acres of land directly behind the Voice of Evangelism. With only 150 people and little income, I prayed, and the Lord said to build a "gathering place for a generation." Thus, we stepped out in faith in the middle of the worst economic recession since the Great Depression, with no bank willing to loan the ministry any money, and needing 12 million additional dollars to pay for this large facility. Joining with the faith of others and praying on a consistent basis, we believed God to send in the money and began building what would become the OCI facility!

HOW THE OCI NAME CAME

God places significance on names, to the point that altars and other places of Divine visitation are often given names. Even the names of key people in the Bible can have prophetic meaning. When we purchased the property for the gathering place, I wanted the right name to be given to the project, the land, and the building. Often a group will sit at a table and "brainstorm" ideas until something clicks. I desired the mind of God as I could see the sovereign hand of the Lord all over what was occurring.

My answer came in Huntington, West Virginia, when one night before service I was asked to meet a young man in his twenties who was autistic and could not speak, instead communicating using a large, flat board with English letters and numbers printed on it. He would whistle with his hand cuffed to his ear, then take his hand and wrap it around his mother's index finger. Pointing to the individual letters, she would spell out the words he wanted to say, then she would communicate them to the person he was speaking to.

His mother told me that this was the way he heard God speaking to him—when he whistled in his ear, then the Lord would impress in his mind what to say. He was so accurate that he could reveal details of a person, their family, or situations that no one knew except the person and God. When he entered the church office with his mother, his mother explained to me about her son Bryan's autism, and how God had spoken to him since he was a child. He then introduced himself, giving me a word he felt the Lord had for me. He tapped out the letters on the wooden board, at times looking up into the air and moving his mother's finger without missing one letter. His mother was his voice and as she explained the words, I could sense his sincerity and discern by what he said that there was accuracy in his revelations. Out of curiosity I asked him some rather strange questions as to what the Lord was telling him about President Obama, and what would happen to the nation (this was in 2010). I was also strongly impressed to ask him in this moment, "What is the Lord's will and His choice in naming the youth ministry facility on the property where I am building the gathering place?"

I saw his eyes tear up as he looked upward, as though he were peering at something in the ceiling. He cupped his hand over his ear and began whistling, like a little bird chirping out a song. He used his mother's index finger and very quickly began pointing to individual letters and she said, "The Lord calls the project 'The Omega Ranch Project.'" I thought to myself, "I like that name. It has a great ring to it." He explained why the Lord chose the name "Omega" for the land and facility. He said, "Jesus is the Alpha and Omega, which are the first and last letters of the Greek alphabet. As the Alpha, He is the *Lamb* of God but as the Omega, is the *Lion* of Judah." At that moment it was as though someone had turned on a light in a dark room. My spirit erupted as I heard the name Omega Center International, which is the meaning of the acronym ,OCI. Since Christ is coming back as a Lion (King) then the word and the Greek letter *Omega* represents Christ's spiritual authority as the *Lion of Judah*! When I first shared the name with some of the youth, they were not that thrilled as they didn't receive the significance of the revelation behind the name. However, this was a "God idea" and I chose to follow God instead of someone else's "good idea."

A BANK DEPOSIT FROM GOD

Once the land was purchased and a building design was drawn, contractors were acquired and the OCI concrete foundation was poured for a 72,000 square foot facility. At that time there were about 50 youth and 50 adults faithfully attending the weekly services. One afternoon, a group gathered at the new property, then placed scriptures in Mezuzah cases in key places within the concrete blocks to ensure the building would be "built on God's Word." Each week a new piece of steel was erected and concrete was poured. Then the need arose for a huge amount of money to begin paying the contractors, as we quickly spent the money that had been set aside for the facility. We needed not hundreds or thousands but millions of dollars. I was not used to praying for money, as during thirty-five years of ministry God had always supplied our ministry needs; but neither had I, in 30 years, constructed any facility costing 18 million dollars! *How do you pray for millions of dollars?* My first revelation was that to God, one dollar or one million dollars is the same, as He is the owner of all things: Thus, it is not too hard for God to supernaturally provide.

I received a revelation that the money must come from someone who has that level of income, but God would need to supernaturally speak to that person. I was impressed to pray for the Lord to "Awaken the spirit of a millionaire," and for God to release to us the money that He had set aside for the purposes of OCI. I will never forget seeing our young people praying on Thursday nights, with one finger pointing into the air, asking God to send us one million dollars. Personally, I did not have any ministry partners, at least to my knowledge, with that type of income. However, our faith was so high and I knew God was directing our future, as it was His vision and not mine. I have often said, "If it is God's will, then it becomes God's bill." This simple phrase lifted the pressure from me and placed the responsibility upon the Lord. I reminded Him that this was His calling, His vision, and His plans; I was just an overseer of this portion of His end-time program.

In July of that year, Susan, the VOE bookkeeper, came to my upstairs office holding something in her hand. Her look was one of both amazement and shock. She said, "Guess what is in my hand." I said, "Is it good or bad," and she replied, "Oh, it is definitely good!" It was a check to our ministry for one million dollars! At that time, the largest donation my ministry had ever received was $280,000. This large donation was very needed for the OCI facility and was a major answer to prayer. That night, I stood up with about 140 people in the small rented building on Old Tasso Road, and said, "Look what the Lord has done!" I flashed on the small screens a copy of the check and the place erupted like a volcano exploding! People were shouting, crying, and even running the aisles. Here was a group that had little income, seeing evidence that God was with us!

Months passed and now our one-million-dollar need had turned into a three-million-dollar need, as the building material and contractors' bills were both piling up at the building site. The prayer team was asking if there were any more special needs, and I said, "Yes, we need three million dollars!" The youth were fired up and said, "Papa, if the Lord can give us one million, why can't He give us three million just as easily?" Their faith was so sincere and pure, and I responded, "Ok, let's pray it in!" We prayed the same prayer, calling in the money assigned to be for our building, reminding God this was His vision, not ours. We again asked Him to "wake up the spirit of a millionaire," as we did not want to go in debt, and had been previously rejected from access to any loans from local banks. We didn't just pray once but many times and on a consistent basis, based on the parable in Luke 18, where the woman continually went before the judge with her need to gain his attention. Eventually, the judge saw the woman's persistence and granted her the petition she desired. We wanted our request to be heard in Heaven, and everyone believed we would again see a financial breakthrough.

One day, I was at the VOE offices and my wife called. Her voice cracked slightly and I could tell she had been crying. She said, "Are you sitting down or standing up?" At first I thought, "Oh no, something bad has happened and she is upset." I asked her the same question that I'd asked my bookkeeper months before, "Is it good or bad news?" Her voice was trembling as she said, "It's good, it's good!" I said, "I'm sitting down, tell me." She replied, "We just received a check from an anonymous contributor through a charitable trust: three million dollars!" I can't remember if I sat there stunned or screamed or jumped up, as this news was a complete shock! I later thought of how our people, just like the disciples, asked God for the impossible and when it occurred both groups were totally surprised, which actually indicates that we didn't really *expect* it to happen but were *hoping* it could happen. After the Apostle James was beheaded, Peter was arrested and sentenced to death when Passover concluded. The church began a continuous prayer marathon, praying nonstop for Peter's release. The angel of the Lord went into the prison at night, releasing Peter and sending him to the prayer meeting. When he knocked on the door, the woman asked who it was and he said, "It's Peter." When she told the people, they did not believe it was him, as they knew he was in jail! They were hoping God would answer their prayer but thought it was Peter's angel! If they'd believed it would happen, they would have opened the door and said, "Glory to God we were expecting you to get out!" (See Acts 12.)

Not only had a total of four million dollars come to the ministry from unknown donors, but when the first of the year arrived another two million came, which was also applied to the OCI building project. In all, people unknown to us were sensitive to the Holy Spirit and sent six million dollars, which allowed us to complete the 72,000 square foot OCI gathering place completely debt free!

One of the reasons we can host Releasing the Roar Conferences, Warrior-Fest, and other major youth events without charging attendance fees is because all of our property, buildings, and equipment are paid in full, and we have no monthly payments owed to any bank! Seeing as God inspired "men to give to our bosom," and He paid for the facility, I would do the Lord a disservice by bringing a generation into a paid building, then require some type of fee to attend. I have many dear friends that must charge a fee, which is perfectly fine, as they have numerous expenses in buildings, P.A. systems, television cameras, and bringing people in for ministry, so that the entrance fees are needed to help pay for expenses.

Late into the building process, I was in prayer and heard this phrase in my spirit: "Where lambs become lions." I had never heard that phrase before, but I knew the concept as the "lambs" would be the younger generation of believers. Sheep would be the adults in the Kingdom and lambs the youth, or the sons and daughters in God's flock. The lion concept is twofold. It refers to *Christ* as the Lion of the tribe of Judah (Rev. 5:5). The lion is also a symbol of the *believer's* authority, as the lion is the king of beasts, symbolizing kingship, a kingdom, strength and authority. OCI's vision remains to train the younger generation to experience God, to walk in His authority, and live in the power of the Holy Spirit!

WHERE LAMBS BECOME LIONS

Personally, I had never heard or researched the name, Warrior-Fest, but I can recall where I was when the name dropped into my spirit. My ministry team and I were sitting on the front row of City Life Church in Tampa, Florida. It was January, and in a few months, the Church of God would be hosting numerous youth conferences across the nation. This church's youth attend one of the main annual events in Knoxville, Tennessee. The youth minister was announcing their plans to take a group to "Winterfest" (a large Church of God youth group gathering). When he said "Winterfest," I literally heard him say "Warrior-Fest!" I turned to my associate and said, "Did you hear that? He said Warrior-Fest," to which my associate responded, "No, he said Winterfest." I whispered back, "He did not." He replied, "Yes, he did." I must have disagreed three or four times, and finally just gave up. Within myself I questioned, "I *know* I heard Warrior-Fest but *why* would I hear Warrior-Fest?" That is when that spark of divine inspiration that occasionally ignites my mind hit me. I mused in my spirit, "It is time you use the OCI facility to reach a generation, for this is the reason it was built, and you should call the gathering, Warrior-Fest!" To confirm this, I thought about our global television program called *Manna-Fest*, a name the Lord spoke to me in 1988 in Florida. Here I was again in Florida with the Holy Spirit giving me another name with "fest"—Warrior-Fest: a meeting "where lambs would become lions!" Everything was coming together and as I told my staff and other spiritual leaders, they all bore witness in their spirits that this was God's will.

We were uncertain how many would attend our first spring

Warrior-Fest but were amazed when 4,100 youth and youth leaders stood in the large OCI hall, worshipping and even sitting on a concrete floor to hear the word of the Lord. The following year, 5,400 were in attendance, and the third year we hosted two Warrior-Fests about two weeks apart, where nearly 10,000 youth and leaders attended at the Omega Ranch and OCI facility. In a total of four events, we have seen about 1800 youth turn their lives over to Christ and over 2,200 baptized in the Holy Spirit. Hundreds have responded to a call of God on their lives for ministry.

The property, building, conferences, and Tuesday night services at OCI were all a result of *one night when the Devil made his biggest mistake: trying to take the life of my son.* We are reaching this generation and you are now alive to be a part of the greatest end-time revival imaginable. Every time you win a person to Christ, see them baptized in the Holy Spirit, or delivered from a bondage, you are making the enemy pay for attacking your generation!

Never let a spiritual battle go to waste. Use what the enemy intended for destruction.

Turn the tables and make him pay by witnessing, praying, winning souls, leading a youth group, starting a Christian band, ministering to drug addicts, hosting youth conferences, or a host of other ministry outreaches. *Snatch the souls of men and women out of the jaws of death and the grip of hell!*

CHAPTER 6

THE PROPHECY OF THE RURAL AWAKENING

A s STATED IN the introduction of this book, this generation is marked with a great promise that no previous generation can claim: The sons and daughters will experience the outpouring of the Spirit and prophesy (Joel 2:29 29). The word *prophesy* can carry various meanings.

One can refer to speaking out and revealing future events (such as the biblical prophets did), and the other to preach or proclaim a particular message God is speaking at that time. Since visions and dreams are also a part of this outpouring, I tend to believe Joel's prediction that sons and daughters will prophesy can refer to both *predicting* and seeing future events (foretelling) and preaching or proclaiming the messages of God and His word (forthtelling).

I began full time ministry at age 18 and for many years have been blessed to experience extended revivals, many of which were initiated by the youth in the church. As the youth began reaching other youth, eventually the fires fanned out and were spread to the parents throughout the church, spreading the flames from the church to the community and throughout surrounding areas. In one Virginia revival, so many kids from the High School were being saved that the drug pushers were having difficulty finding young people to whom they could traffic drugs. However, I recognize that Joel's promised outpouring is much larger in scale than one area, and will spread to all ethnic groups ("all flesh") very swiftly, as the prophet used the phrase "pour out." This phrase is similar to a person who purposely and quickly pours water from a vessel, or to a rainstorm where the water is falling from the sky with such force, it is called an "outpouring." Since this outpouring is universal, diverse, and on the youth, how will this revival be initiated? I have always felt it would be more sovereign and supernatural than planned and strategized by men. God moves spontaneously, as indicated on the Day of Pentecost when, "Suddenly, there came a sound from heaven ..." (Acts 2:2).

At some point, the youth themselves must seize the moment, uniting themselves as a "Kingdom army." They must seek the Lord to initiate a soul-winning spiritual outpouring, without waiting for a particular revivalist or evangelist to arrive in town, sparking a series of protracted church meetings that break out into what we traditionally call a revival. The youth must become the voices, carry the anointing, and become the God-ordained ministers of their own revivals.

You may ask, "What can I do, as just one person, without a larger group backing me up?" There is a young girl, who lives in a Communist nation, where Christianity is banned and any believer persecuted and jailed if discovered. At the time this information was leaked out of the nation by missionaries who personally met her, she was 16 years of age and had made her way into a secret location in a jungle to share her testimony. One of my personal missionary friends, Rusty "blue flame" Dominque, was in the meeting. This girl has over 20,000 converts and does not have a church building but meets in caves, the back of covered trucks, and the jungle to hide from the Communist authorities. She will go on 21 day fasts, then find a small village and begin praying for the sick, or more incredibly, raising the dead! She only does what is led by the Spirit, after long fasts and days of prayer.

On one occasion, she went into a small area of a town (what we'd call the town square) and began asking if there was anyone who had recently died. There was one man who had already been wrapped in a mat and laid in the ground. She requested to bring him out of his burial place. She would pray and God would raise him from the dead. They mocked her and refused, but that night, while the people slept, she went to the spot and drug the man with the bamboo mat into the town square. When the sun came up, there she was, sitting beside the dead man. The townspeople gathered in the square, yelled at her, and were going to kill her for disturbing the dead. She replied, "I will pray to my God, the living God, and He will raise him from the dead as a sign to all of you. If this does not happen, then you can kill me." She began praying earnestly, loudly and boldly, when suddenly the man's body began to move. After a few moments, he was breathing and his eyes opened! The people were in great fear and shock, and began to believe she was some god among them. She preached Christ to them, and that day another town was added to the Kingdom of God! *This is not something an average believer just goes and does*, or should attempt to try haphazardly, as she fasts for weeks, spends hours and days in prayer, and God uses her to prove to atheists that He is real.

When Rusty met her, he wanted to take a picture with her. As he stood there, he felt massive conviction and heard an inner voice say, "You are not worthy to get in a picture with her!" Rusty fell on his knees and began crawling away. Here was a girl that had no band, no church building, no PA system or pews, just the basics: prayer, fasting, and a word from the Lord. Despite her lack of traditional ideas of church, God is using her in a nation that despises Christianity and arrests Christians.

THE COAL FIELD REVIVAL

In the past when men such as Billy Graham preached revivals, the meetings were conducted in tents, stadiums, or auditoriums in large cities where massive crowds of people could attend. At times, Billy preached outdoors with huge crowds packed together like sardines, standing on roads and sidewalks. During "the Healing Revival" from 1948 to 1955, the tents were placed in suburban Southern and Midwestern cities, with roads, hotels, and gas stations to accommodate the thousands driving into the area to attend the services. During my season, the revivals that continued for many weeks included Pulaski, Virginia; Dalton, Georgia; Daisy and Lafollette,

Tennessee; Gainesville, Georgia; and other small-to medium-populated towns in the southeast. For years, I questioned how God would use the youth to launch the Joel 2 revival.

Years ago, I was driving through the area of Norton, Virginia, on my way to visit places where my father began his ministry in McDowell County, West Virginia. The towns were once booming communities in the 1950s and '60s when the coal mines and companies were strong, and the miners were being paid well for performing very dangerous jobs. Eventually, due to liberal politics and new government regulations from extreme environmental laws, the coal mines began closing while some politicians bragged about how they would shut down the coal industry. As I drove through the small town, I could sense the depression, poverty, and feeling of isolation that was hovering over many of the rural towns. I also saw many young people walking the streets or just loafing around on the sidewalks, and I knew they were living under a spirit of hopelessness. This image was burned in my mind and I have never been able to get away from it. These were Virginia and West Virginia towns where I began preaching in small, rural churches many years ago.

My own father was converted to the Lord in the late 1940s when a woman minister named Mildred Collins began preaching in small, mountain churches in McDowell County, West Virginia, initiating a revival that continued for forty-two months. Over seventy young men were converted to the Lord in that revival and all of them, according to my father, eventually entered some form of ministry. Years before my father's death, he bought a house, and later a small trailer, outside of War, West Virginia, where he prayed for two things: that his brother Morgan would come back to the Lord before he passed away and that God would send another revival to the coal fields! Dad remembered how this coal field revival came as the result of a few men and women joining to pray each evening for six consecutive months, crying out for God to send a revival to the area. It did come, and although it was never listed in Charismatic or Pentecostal history among the noted outpourings such as the Parham Revival, Azusa Street in Los Angeles, or the Murphy outpouring that led to the formation of the Church of God, it impacted several counties for years. The revival brought lasting fruit by converting hardened miners to Christ, delivering men from alcoholism, and helping men to be faithful to their wives and families.

THE RURAL AWAKENING

In August 2015, I was ministering at Christ Temple Church in Huntington, West Virginia, during a conference we host each year. It was a Sunday night service, and the Holy Spirit was changing my thoughts on the message I was to preach. I stood before a packed sanctuary of spiritually hungry men, women, and youth, preparing to minister when suddenly I felt the atmosphere "shift," the presence of the Lord surrounding me. It felt like electricity jumping in the air, and I stood perfectly still and silent for a moment, feeling as though I was going into some type of "trance," which is a feeling where you are caught up in the Spirit. I began to sense a prophetic word was about to be released, and in my mind asked the Lord to take direction of the service and flow as He desired.

Suddenly, the Holy Spirit began to reveal that a major event would happen in America that would get the attention of the nation, and that sinners would not discern it as a message from the Lord, while discerning believers would. The Spirit then revealed there would be a time when people would begin to leave cities and move into the more rural areas, partially for the safety of their families.

To me, the most interesting part of the prophecy was when the Spirit revealed that a revival known as the "rural revival" was on its way. This revival would come into selected areas where the people were hungry and had been praying for a great move of God. Within seven months after receiving this word, I began hearing of revival where hundreds of people were being converted in parts of West Virginia. There were initially 300 mostly young people converted and weeks later, several thousand throughout one county had come to Christ. As other youth have attended these revivals, the fire of God has struck them and the revival has spread to other regions. One group in a farming community began in a small church, later moved to another church and outgrowing it, eventually put up a tent with 1,200 in attendance. In a revival in North Carolina, over 5,000 attended under a huge tent cathedral, with hundreds standing outside. In other small towns, extended revivals have become common. The evangelists are not silver-tongued orators trained in Ivy League classrooms, with professors of religion assisting the preaching student on how to stand, breathe, and use their hands when delivering a sermon. These are unknown sons and daughters, who do not care whether their face appears on a poster or television. They are spreading the revival fire, leading an awakening in the mountains and hills of rural America.

GOD MOVES IN UNUSUAL PLACES

Prior to Christ being revealed as the Messiah and beginning his public ministry, He was baptized in the Jordan River by his cousin, John the Baptist. John's birth had been announced thirty years prior by the angel Gabriel, who predicted his name would be John and that he would come "in the spirit and power of Elijah" (Luke 1:17). The angel also said that John's ministry would "turn the hearts of the fathers to the children." This phrase was an amazing 400 years-old prediction made by the prophet Malachi, who said God would "send Elijah the prophet...to turn the hearts of the fathers to the children and the heart of the children to their fathers" (Mal. 4:5-6).

John was in a desolate desert. God knew in advance that the center of the revival could not break out in Jerusalem, as there were so many differing sects (the Pharisees, Sadducees, Herodians, Zealots, etc.) keeping the religious pot stirred up in Jerusalem. John's father, Zacharias, was a priest in the temple, wearing the priestly garments and eating the kosher food while performing daily rituals. Yet, John did not initiate his call to repentance in Jerusalem. First, most of Jerusalem's religious leaders would have rejected his "repent and be baptized" message, as they had huge pools of water (called mikvahs) outside the city walls in which they disrobed and submerged before entering the temple. This ritual bath ceremonially "sanctified" them before entering the sacred enclosure. To the Pharisees, they were already law abiders, clean and following God, so John's message would have fallen on deaf ears in the holy city.

Instead, John went into the heart of Judea, into the "Judean wilderness," a very dry, hot, rocky, and in some places, barren region with one main water source—the Jordan River. There were only some small "rural" villages in the area, but when John began preaching and baptizing, the people came out of the cities to the wilderness where he resided! This proves that when God ordains a revival or spiritual awakening, you don't need a big church, a large city, a great band, and entertainment to hold the crowd. You just need prayer, preaching, and the power of conviction from the Holy Spirit!

John, called by theologians "John the Baptist" or "John the Baptizer," would possibly have been banned from the Temple because of his appearance. The Bible says John wore a camel's hair garment and a leather belt, eating locust and wild honey (Matt. 3:4). In Jerusalem, the priests (preachers) were required to wear white linen robes when ministering in the temple and, of course, there were certain restrictions placed upon them according to the law and traditions of the priesthood. Imagine John walking onto the outer Temple platform, dressed in rough camel's hair with some sticky honey clinging to his face and a few locust legs sticking out from between his teeth, screaming at the top of his lungs, "Repent you generation of vipers and hypocrites; how shall you escape the wrath of God which is coming!" (Luke 3:7). I believe they would have reached for rocks to stone him; after all, that was their response to Jesus at the temple when he demanded the same two-faced religious hypocrites to repent (see John 10).

There is a threefold point to be made from the John the Baptist narrative. *First, he came in the "spirit of Elijah" to turn the hearts of a generation,* removing the generational gap between the spiritual fathers and sons. John's father was a priest, automatically placing John in the position of a priest, as the priesthood was hereditary, not a chosen occupation. This father-son team was totally opposite as one was in Jerusalem and the other in the wilderness; one wore soft, white clothes and the other (John) very rugged attire. According to Jewish tradition, this was the type of garment that the real prophet Elijah wore, and before being caught up to heaven Elijah left his garment and belt here on earth where it was later concealed in a side cabinet in the golden altar. This may be why knowledgeable Jews questioned if John was the prophet Elijah, as John was now dressed as Elijah from centuries before. John told them he was not Elijah but was the "voice crying in the wilderness" (see John 1:21-32).

The "spirit of Elijah" does not refer to the actual spirit from the physical body of Elijah coming into John the Baptist, but refers to the anointing and various characteristics of Elijah re-emerging through John the Baptist. Elijah was fiery, bold and uncompromising, just as John was. When we speak of the end-time revival that is now upon the earth and the "spirit of Elijah," we are not just speaking of fire and boldness, but also of the fact that this anointing will awaken the "children" (sons and daughters) and unite them with spiritual parents. This final end-time revival must have the same fire, boldness, power, authority, and uniting of the generations that occurred through the John-the-Baptist/Elijah anointing.

*The **second** point is that John did not dress or look in any way "traditional."* His clothes were rough, and preaching in the hot sun made his skin look tanned and perhaps a bit leathery; his personality was blunt and to the point. In this revival, the youth will not necessarily have the "church look" that many people are used to, which is a pattern for the coming "John the Baptist generation" that will also operate in the boldness of the "spirit of Elijah."

When my dad was called to preach, a minster was required to wear a suit and tie in all church settings and religious functions. At times, the "country preacher" wore just a white cotton shirt with an open collar, as there was no air conditioning in the churches and in the summer the small sanctuaries could feel like a sauna. When I began my ministry, I always wore a white shirt and tie; but as years passed, I went to a high-collared golf shirt and a jacket, as this was far more comfortable to preach in. I remember preaching large camp meetings dressed this way, at times people looking at me as though I was half-naked because the tie was missing. I never made a public comment about it but continued to preach, and this style eventually came to be known as "business casual." Some churches still like their minister to dress formally on Sunday morning and if I am ministering in a more traditional setting, I will follow their tradition; otherwise, you will find me in "business casual," or in a youth setting, in jeans and a special shirt. My son, however, always wears jeans and a nice t-shirt to church, as he works in the sound booth. In this final move, people should not stare down individuals to see how a person is dressed, as this makes people feel others are judging them.

I recall in 1980, I was in Alabama inviting unsaved people to attend a church where I was preaching a revival. In that day, female church members were forbidden from wearing any jeans or pants to church, only dresses. One young unsaved girl was interested in coming, but she said, "I really cannot attend church there, because I know all the girls wear dresses and I do not own one." That's when it hit me; if people were not normally church attendees or they worked in a "blue-collar" industry, they might not own what was considered "proper". I discovered many women would not attend a classical Pentecostal church because they felt they would be judged and stared down by others if they walked in the door; and to be honest, this statement may not be far from the truth. It was similar with men. In that day, most men wore a suit and tie to church. However, recent surveys show that 80% of men do not even own or wear a suit. Dressing up is nice, looks good, and is perhaps respectful; but what about the people who don't have the clothes or are uncomfortable dressing up? Are we just going to let them die lost because of their appearance? It would do well to remember that Jesus wore a robe and sandals into the synagogue: no socks, just sandals. I wonder what would happen if a pastor went to his pulpit barefoot except for a small leather sole held by sewn leather straps under his feet?

In this revival, people will not be judged by the style of their clothes, the color of their hair, or how they look outwardly, as "man looks upon the outward appearance but God looks upon the heart" (1 Sam. 16:7). We don't always know people's personal reasons for doing what they do. I knew of a woman who was often teased and at times mocked for the wigs she wore. What few people knew was that she had a gene that caused her natural hair to become thin, forcing her to wear a wig because of her situation. She suffered undue criticism and never publically told of her genetic challenge.

*The **third** and very important point is that John the Baptist was a single, young man who headed up this "Wilderness Revival."* I have been to Israel over 34 times and have stood on the banks of the Jordan River at John's traditional baptismal site. The river is about 50 feet wide and rather muddy, with reeds growing from the mud-caked banks. For miles, all you can see is dry, desolate land, with the exception of Jericho, a beautiful oasis with palm trees and numerous homes and buildings, today a popular tourist destination. Yet, people came from the towns and cities to a dry wilderness to hear John preach and to be baptized by him. It was not John's appearance or personality that attracted the multitudes but his message and anointing. The yoke-breaking, soul-saving, devil-chasing anointing of the Holy Spirit will still attract attention and bring people to Christ!

Just as people "came to the middle of nowhere" to see and hear John, causing them to repent and be baptized, the Holy Spirit will continue to break out in pockets of revival and selective outpouring in the mountains! Remember, John's mom and dad were from the "hill country" of Judea (Luke 1:39-40), where small communities were scattered about and homes were built around springs of water. God loves the mountains! Noah's Ark rested on Mount Ararat; God gave the Law in a desert on a mountain called Sinai; Elijah prayed the fire down on Mount Carmel; and Jesus went up into a high mountain to pray, the same mountain on which he was transfigured, later dying on a hill known in Hebrew as Golgotha!

God's throne sits on what is called Mount Zion; Jerusalem is surrounded by seven mountains; the hill where the Temple once sat is called "the Holy Mountain."

In my earlier ministry, my revivals would often continue in local churches, averaging two to three weeks in length. Some went as long as eleven weeks, with preaching each night. The revivals that birthed the greatest results were the churches in smaller, rural towns in the southeast. The fire spread faster through word of mouth, and when a notable conversion or miracle occurred, the unsaved or backslidden would be pulled into the revival anointing like a magnet.

6 REASONS A RURAL AWAKENING WILL OCCUR

I want to briefly give you, six reasons a rural awakening will occur. Although there may be many more reasons, these are the main six that I sense in my spirit.

First, this awakening will occur because of countless "prayer seeds" that have been sown during previous generations. Over many, many years, small remnants of faithful prayer warriors have cried out to God from the mountains, pleading for the Almighty to send a revival to their towns and regions. This type of intercession can extend for months or even years before the actual breakthrough is experienced. My Father, who was converted during the Coal Field Revival in the late 1940s, purchased a small home in McDowell County, and as he got older would spend hours every day seeking God for revival. His prayers, along with others who are now gone, are the seeds, their tears are the water, and their zeal the soil required for an eventual harvest of souls.

Cornelius was an Italian Gentile who gave to the poor and prayed continually. One day, an angel came to him saying that his "prayers and charitable giving have come up before God as a memorial" (Acts 10:1-4). The phrase "prayers have come up" is interesting, as in the book of Revelation, the prayers of believers are stored in "prayer bowls," ensuring that all prayers believers have ever prayed are preserved and reserved in the temple in Heaven, before God's throne. At "appointed" or "set" times, these prayers bowls are opened or "tipped over" (as some suggest); when the words come before God, He immediately sends the answers to those prayers back to Earth. This is exactly what occurred with Cornelius. Prayers for revival may appear to be unheard, as often in a community things continue as normal without any visible soul harvest. However, true revivals are set in God's timing, as I will explain in a bit.

There is a well-known, female minister whose ministry has influenced tens of thousands. She can recall as a young girl being placed in a small room with her grandmother, whom the family kept locked up in a room because they believed her to be "crazy." When her grandmother saw her, she would pick her up and rock her in a rocking chair, mumbling strange words over her. This went on continually throughout her elementary school years. After some time, she received Christ, was called into the ministry, and began to identify the "truth" about her grandmother: She was a woman who read the Bible and believed in God. She was actually praying over her in that rocking chair, and other members of the family just thought she was a nut. God heard granny's prayers though they tried to shut her up!

The **second** *reason is that the rural churches have shown themselves as some of the most steadfast in remaining loyal to God* in good and bad times, staying faithful in small things. In Revelation, Christ spoke to a faithful church and told them, "I have set before you an open door, and no man can shut it: for you have a little strength, and have kept my word and not denied it." I am told most churches in America average about 75 on Sunday morning, and there are tens of thousands of churches this size scattered throughout the small towns of America. Oftentimes these churches will have little emphasis on the youth, whether due to budget issues or because the focus is on keeping the older members happy.

However, God has seen the faithfulness of the small remnant groups, specifically the ones that have prayed and sought Him with heavy burdens for souls. There is a spiritual principle in the Word, spoken when Christ said, "If you are faithful over a few things I will make you ruler over many" (Matt. 25:21). God is not looking for a great set of brains, charismatic personality, or charm. He is looking for obedience and faithfulness.

The **third** *reason is that a spirit of hopelessness often leads people to turn to God.* Many of my family are originally from West Virginia, my dad and his family having grown up in the heart of the coal fields in Bartly, West Virginia. Many years ago, the coal industry was booming with economic growth, and many foreign individuals arrived in America to work in the West Virginia and Kentucky mines. Eventually, due to environmental concerns (actually some environmental extremists), the federal government began placing unbelievable pressure and regulations on the mines. Some politicians even said they would work to shut down the coal industry entirely. This occurrence caused the loss of thousands of mining jobs, as well as other jobs connected with the industry. The once-active main street shops in the small towns are now abandoned buildings, and beautiful homes empty and overrun with weeds consuming their front lawns.

While older people can retire and reflect on better days in the past, the younger generation often has no motivation for the future. This creates a void, an emotional and spiritual emptiness, that often leads to sexual immorality, drug and alcohol addiction, or petty crime. The root is what I call a "spirit of hopelessness." In ancient Israel, the people would prosper and forget God, then over time be turned over to an enemy which would lead them into economic weakness and spiritual bondage, causing individuals to cry out to God for help. This occurred when the Egyptian government forced the Hebrew people into slavery, baking bricks and building treasure cities for the Pharaohs. When the people cried out unto the Lord in unison, He heard them and "remembered His covenant" (Exod. 2:24). God initiated the Exodus, breaking the yoke of Egypt, bringing His people into their Promised Land.

Many areas of our nation have been hit with economic downturns, especially the coal fields and small-town America. However, just as God remembered His covenant with His people, He will remember the prayers and hear the heart cries of all people that feel trapped in a cycle of poverty and injustice. We are uncertain how long the Hebrews groaned in their slavery before Moses was raised up as a deliverer. Remember, Moses spent forty years in a desert (there's that desert again) then met God, hearing his voice from a burning bush on a mountain (Exod. 3:1-2). In fact, Moses' encounter was on the "backside" of the mountain (Exod. 3:1). Have you ever heard someone call another person "backwards," meaning they are shy or socially withdrawn? I remember some of the more "refined" Christian's once looked at me and bestowed the title "Hillbilly Preacher". I told them I was actually more comfortable among the hill people than I was around their stiff necks!

When people have no one and nowhere else to turn, they will many times repent and turn to God when confronted with a message of hope, peace, and joy through a redemptive covenant. The Lord will respond by sending His delivering power and His presence to them.

*The **fourth** reason revival will come is to fulfill a promise given to the Biblical prophets.* Several prophets in Scripture refer to a time when the Holy Spirit will be greatly active on the earth. Joel penned the most detailed prediction, that God would pour out His Spirit upon all flesh and the sons and daughters would prophesy (Joel 2:28-29). This prediction was also repeated by Peter on the Day of Pentecost, when the Spirit was poured out and the church was formed (Acts 2:17-17). Its fulfillment will be "in the last days" (Acts 2:17) and "before the great and terrible day of the Lord," which is the future Great Tribulation (Joel 2:31). Numerous biblical signs necessary to unfold before the Lord's return have been, and are being, fulfilled in our time. There is also evidence that the

Tribulation lies just over the horizon; thus, the timing is perfect for this spiritual outpouring to be unleashed upon the earth.

To me this is an important point—God cannot lie! When God makes a promise it will occur, perhaps not in our timing but definitely in His. I repeat what I said earlier: This is a generation with an amazing promise and the question is not, *will God send* the outpouring but *will you participate* in it? Will you *get in* on the *pouring out?*

Fifth, today's younger generation is open to the filling and gifts of the Holy Spirit while the older may resist due to erroneous teaching and resistance to Him. I believe this is a unique and important reason God will send this final blast of His presence to the sons and daughters. In over 40 years of evangelizing America, I have observed that the older generation is often "set in their ways" and certainly does not like any type of change from their traditions or routines. If they do not believe that God heals the sick in this age, that miracles were a blessing only for New Testament times, or that speaking in tongues and other vocal gifts have ceased, then it is often difficult to change their minds. As some have told me, "I've lived this long without speaking in tongues so why should I asked God for the gift now?" The point is, God cannot fill a human vessel with His Spirit if that *vessel has the lid sealed tight* and won't allow the rivers of living water to flow through them (see John 7:38-39). Some people are so anti-Holy Spirit that they borderline on blaspheming Him with their words. In 1978, I was preaching in Richmond, Virginia when a revival broke out in the

Christian School. The Father of one of the students was a board member at a local Church of Christ, a denomination that taught any form of speaking in other tongues in the church today was a demonic delusion. His daughter had gone home and told her dad the Spirit of God had touched her. He exploded in anger, went to the principal of the Christian school and said, "I would rather have my daughter die and go to hell than to have her claim to have this so-called baptism of the Holy Ghost."

Many of today's youth are illiterate in the Bible, having little spiritual understanding, which makes them more open to receive revelation and insight than perhaps their parent's or grandparent's generations. Earlier in my ministry, it was quite a challenge to preach on the outpouring of the Holy Spirit, as few of the mainline Christian branches of the church were open to this doctrine. Forty years later, however, we often see hundreds receive the Holy Spirit in just one service! The great and final latter rain coming to the earth will be focused upon young men and women, as they tend to be less traditionally stuck in one frame of thought and are more open to the truths found in the Scriptures.

The **sixth** *reason for this rural awakening will be that God is waiting until this time to remove the various forms of legalism* that could hinder converts from coming to Christ by rejection from the legalistic, "holiness" church. When I was growing up, there was an emphasis on linking a person's holiness to their outward appearance: short hair for men, long hair and no make-up or jewelry for women, as this was considered an outward sign of a person's level of holiness. However, this led to church members viewing people outwardly to determine their spirituality; thus, if you looked "right" on the outside, you must be "right" on the inside. This is what the Pharisees believed; but Jesus told them while outside they were perfect, whitewashed tombs, inside they were full of dead men's bones just like the tombs in Jerusalem. This means their outward righteousness was filthy and useless because their hearts were not pure before God. Judging outwardly led to "legalism." Legalism has different definitions: one being when Christians place improper or excessive emphasis (outside the boundaries of the actual Scripture) on certain rules or traditions in order to attain salvation.

As an example, when I began my ministry in Virginia in 1977, some ministers told me not to wear a colored shirt or a red tie. A few would not allow me to preach in their church, as my hair was touching my ears. There is nothing at all about colored clothing (including red) or length of hair (in fact, look at Samson!) in Scripture. These things are preferences, not doctrine. Yet in my early ministry, if anyone came into the church not having their outward appearance in line with the church's traditions, they were not welcomed and usually were never to return to that church again.

Years ago, I realized the "root" cause of all legalism dwelled in the denominations pushing church *membership* above personal *discipleship*. I'm not being critical here, just honest. The pastor's and leading bishop's salaries and financial benefits were set according to the number of members in a church or state. Thus, more members meant tithers, and tithers meant more income. Tithes are biblical, but trying to get members just for tithes is "putting the cart before the horse."

I saw how discipleship was put on the backburner with my own eyes. Years ago, I returned from a revival and went to the state evangelism director to report that several Methodist ladies received the Holy Spirit baptism. He smiled and instead of rejoicing said, "Did you take them as members into the church?" I just stared at him. On another occasion, I was in a five-week revival and had over 152 souls saved with actual altar cards containing their names and information. I remember the pastor, who was in his early sixties, looked at the cards, then at me, and said, "If these people don't join the church I would rather not even have them coming. It's just more work for me and it won't help my monthly salary unless they join." I am so glad 90% of the ministers and churches did not think this way, but it was quite discouraging. Jesus did not say, "Go into the entire world and make church members," but he did say, "Go into the entire world and make disciples." In the earlier days, it seemed some churches wanted to make clones (people who looked, talked, and acted like them) and not disciples. A disciple is a follower of Christ and His teachings.

FYI: It is biblical to give tithe (the tenth of your income) and offerings, and also to be added to a local church roster and get involved in their ministry. However, the purpose of the church is to create disciples, and be a center for love—not to create a hoard of legalistic clones. I have seen five and six thousand young people in one building, and they seldom ask each other, "What denomination are you with?" Instead, they are packed wall to wall in the big hall, hands raised, worshipping together.

WHY GOD WAITS

Great outpourings are prayed into existence and aligned with the harvest seasons. Not all spiritual harvest fields are ripe at the same time. In Israel, barley ripens in early spring, wheat is not ready until the early summer, and olives in the early fall. Herein is an important point about the timing of the rural awakening.

If the Lord had sent a major awakening in the earlier days, the members of the local church may not have been ready to receive the appearance of the young people coming into the building! The kids are coming in with holes in their jeans, rainbow colored hair, tattoos, and piercings covering their face. In my early days, these kids would have been met at the altar by a few well-meaning saints. After "praying them through," they'd have said, "Now that you are saved, get that dye out of your hair, don't come back in with those ugly jeans, cover those tattoos, and be sure to remove that silver stuff hanging from your nose and ears—*then* the Lord will be pleased." This would have run most of the youth off and killed the revival. God patiently waited until some time passed for the church to be receptive to sinners before allowing the Body of Christ to move into a soul-winning revival.

Remember, it was God who said that an entire generation would die in the wilderness before the forty and under crowd of Hebrews could enter the Promised Land. Only two older men, Joshua who was 80 and Caleb who was 85, were permitted to lead the next generation of people into the land. For Israel, it took a forty-year process for God to change their thinking, from an Egyptian mentality to an Israelite mentality. They came out of Egypt thinking like slaves, evolved in the wilderness to understand they were

God's sons, and by the time the youth were raised up, were soldiers ready to war against the enemy and seize back lost territory to claim their inheritance.

In the church, we have taught the blessing of being sons and daughters, but some have refused to go to war, becoming complacent and settling into their padded pews. It is time for you to rise up, put on the armor of God, and prepare for war: not a political revolution such as some are attempting to organize, but a nonviolent prayer, fasting, and worship revolution, raising up an end-time army, ready to take back souls from the grip of Satan and wreak havoc on the kingdom of darkness

WHAT DETERMINES REVIVAL?

In summary, what determines revival in some areas when other areas are in spiritual drought? One obscure verse may help answer this question:

> "And also I have withheld the rain from you, when there were yet three months to the harvest: and I caused it to rain upon one city, and caused it not to rain upon another city: one piece was rained upon, and the piece whereupon it rained did not wither. So two or three cities wandered unto one city, to drink water..."
>
> – Amos 4:7-8

Perhaps you have heard of the Brownsville revival that continued for years in Pensacola, Florida. I am close friends with John Kilpatrick, who pastored at Brownsville when the revival broke out. He preached at OCI and explained that two years before the revival he set up different banners, each with a different focus, and set people to praying continually for revival. At the same time, there was a prophecy by South Korean Pastor David Yonggi Cho that "God would send a revival to the seaside city of Pensacola and it will spread like fire until all of America will be consumed by God." The revival erupted on Father's Day, Sunday morning June 18, 1995, at the Brownsville Assembly of God with Steve Hill. The power of God struck the place, bringing the fire and anointing that led to a mighty outpouring. It was said as many as four million people attended and over 200,000 were converted to Christ! Thus, the "rain of the Spirit" drenched this one city, and since many surrounding cities were not experiencing this same outpouring, many thirsty individuals traveled long distances to enjoy the "Pensacola Outpouring!" According to Amos, it is God who chooses where to send the rain, as some areas are more "thirsty and prepared" than others.

An evangelist since age 18, I can suggest why revival comes to some areas while others remain dry:

1. Revival is released according to the level of prayer from a specific area

2. Revival is released due to the extreme spiritual needs of an area or a nation

3. Revival is released when there is an intense hunger and thirst for more of God

4. Revival is released when God finds a people ready to take on the weight of a revival

Revival does not happen by accident or chance. The seeds of prayer are sown into the heavens, heaven receives them and in turn, the harvest is a revival of souls. The soil of the heart must be softened with the water of the tears of believers, and the light of the Word must warm the human spirit as the truth is preached, setting people free. Revival is prayed down with holy fire and not worked up with human emotion. Revival is coming and the question is: Will you dive into the river headfirst or remain on the side watching while others flow with the current of the outpouring that is here and is coming?

CHAPTER SEVEN

IT JUST TAKES A LITTLE TO MAKE A BIG DIFFERENCE

O NE DAY I was thinking about all of the miracles that are alluded to in the Bible. At that moment, I realized we often emphasize the faith and obedience of the person receiving the miracle of deliverance, without noting the "little things" that, if omitted, would have radically changed the story.

Without a dead tree branch (the rod) in the hands of Moses, the children of Israel may have been stuck at the Red Sea unable to cross. The crafter of the slingshot used by David when swinging a rock at Goliath was never named, but without the sling made of wood, the miracle would have never occurred. Some unknown person sowed a seamless garment for Christ to wear: a garment that the sick touched as a point of contact for their miracles.

Someone had to make the handkerchiefs over which Paul prayed and were handed to the sick, causing demons to exit the possessed and the sick to be healed. Thus, when we recall any miracle from the Bible, we focus on the giver and receiver, the person praying and the person receiving. In reality, without the unnamed persons linked to the rod, the garment, the sling, the handkerchiefs, or the "little things", the outcomes of the stories may not have been the same. As people have said for years, "It is the little things that count."

Remember this: Everyone starts out with little.

YOUR GREATEST FEAR

What do you think the greatest fear throughout life is? Three common answers are usually expressed:

1. The fear of death

2. The fear of financial loss

3. The fear of a major sickness or lost loved ones

My personal observation is that the single greatest fear throughout life is the fear of failure — or falling flat on our faces and not succeeding.

Here is a list of men who "failed" initially. The poet Carl Sandburg flunked English at West Point. Albert Einstein didn't begin talking until age 3 and failed his first college exam. He never learned to drive a car and was once given a $1,500 check, used it as a bookmark, then lost the book! The famous movie actor

Clark Gable failed at his first screen test because his ears were too big. Henry Ford of car industry fame wanted to sell watches, but instead made automobiles—and forgot to put a reverse gear in his first car. Thomas Edison failed 1,000 times to invent the light bulb. When reminded how many times he had failed, he said, "I didn't fail 1,000 times; I succeeded once!" Thomas Jefferson suffered migraines all his life and took 18 days to write the Declaration of Independence. President Andrew Johnson didn't learn to read and write until he was a married man. The famous writer, Edgar Allen Poe, took ten years to write his bestselling book, *The Raven*, and only received $10.00 for the manuscript; he was expelled from West Point in 1831 and so poor he once ate dandelions for nine days.

Another man, whose entire life seemed like one failure after another, is a major example of how suddenly something can turn around. He was born on a farm in Indiana in 1890. His father died when he was 5 and his mother had to work for the family peeling tomatoes. As a child, he had to assist in cooking for his smaller siblings. He left school in 6th grade to work on the farm full time; his mother sent him back to Indiana at age 12, where he worked as a farmhand for $15.00 a month because he was unable to get along well with his step-father. He joined the military. From 1915-1920, he took a job practicing law but was charged with assault after getting in a fight with a client in the courtroom. He eventually married and divorced, moving to three states during this time. He held many jobs and attempted to start a company that eventually went out of business. In 1920, he moved to Corbin, Kentucky to start a restaurant and a gas station for travelers. He had one table and six chairs. In 1939, he started a restaurant chain that failed.

One day he came up with an idea that would change his life. He came up with a pressure cooker that could cook chicken in 9 minutes, and began to sell chicken that became a hit with travelers. In 1956, the government made a road that bypassed his restaurant and he was almost broke by age 66. However, he came up with special spices and continued cooking chicken. The popularity of his chicken expanded from one location throughout the United States. In 1986, the Pepsi Company bought out his restaurant chain for $840 million dollars!

This man was Colonel Harlan Sanders, and his restaurant Kentucky Fried Chicken. His life proves that we all have times when our plans may fail; but failure is not final, and you must continue pressing forward, not looking back to dwell on things that didn't work out. It's not how you start but how you finish that counts.

I STARTED WITH NOTHING BUT FAITH

Today our ministry consists of three major branches. The first is the Voice of Evangelism International Ministry, which is impacting the world with seven outreaches. The second branch is the OCI ministry, consisting of a fellowship of believers meeting each Tuesday night, a youth emphasis, and now hosting numerous, major conferences throughout the year. The third and newest outreach is our ISOW (International School of the Word) Internet Bible School.

The ministry also owns five separate facilities that are used for ministry on our property, including locations in the county. Our VOE and OCI properties total over 100 acres and are continually being developed for new lodges, future camp facilities, and school dorms and buildings. The ministry buildings have the finest state-of-the-art equipment for sound and video recording, assisting us in our outreaches. All of the ministry assets, land, building, equipment and so forth, is about 25 million dollars, debt free. What is amazing is that all of this we see today began with one 32-page book I wrote when I was 18 years of age.

My goal for a book outreach was never to "build a global ministry," but my heart and my purpose were to reach people beyond the pulpit. I discovered early that if I only reached people that personally attended my revivals, I would be very limited in winning the lost and teaching valuable spiritual truths to others. Thus, I traded my drum set to a printer, who printed 500 copies of my first, 32-page book, *Precious Promises for Believers.* They sold for $1 a copy. That simple booklet went places I could not go and was read by people that I had not met, even passing from person to person. This initiated several more books. Eventually my revival sermons were taped on cassette tape and sold in revivals. Those unable to attend could order the messages through the ministry. At first, there were perhaps five to fifteen orders a week coming in the mail, being processed and fulfilled in the basement of our home. Over time, prophetic videos were produced in a simple studio and these too were offered in meetings, over television specials, and in a small publication I was printing, called *The Voice of Evangelism Magazine.* These outreaches seemed to emerge over time and flowed into other forms, but my goal remained the same:

reach as many people as possible with the messages and teaching material. Reaching North America and the world was the ultimate reason for the weekly *Manna-Fest* telecast, as this program could go into nations and be viewed by individuals I would never meet in this life.

My point is this: Our global ministry didn't just descend from heaven and drop into my office like the New Jerusalem when it comes down from Heaven to Earth. It was birthed and matured to what it is today. A ministry is similar to a child; it must be birthed, nourished, protected, directed and grown.

The spiritual principle here is that from a small seed (one 32-page booklet) emerged a major outreach ministry! God always begins with small things and, eventually, He enlarges and grows them. An example is the nation of Israel. In Hebrew, the name Israel is spelt with a *yud* (י) which is the smallest letter of the Hebrew alphabet and ends with *lamed* (ל) which is the tallest letter of the alphabet. To rabbis this indicates that Israel would begin as the smallest of nations but grow great in the earth to become the largest of nations. This reminds me of a line from an old song that said, "Little is much when God is in it."

Lot was spared by moving in the direction of a "little city" when Sodom was destroyed (Gen. 19:20). Saul, Israel's first king, was from the tribe of Benjamin, which was the smallest among Israel's twelve tribes (1 Sam. 9:21). David was the youngest of his brothers. And Christ was from Nazareth, a very small town in the upper Galilee, considered so little in population and significance that people said, "Can any good thing come out of Nazareth?" (John 1:46).

Often a young person will say, "I am just *one person* and I can't do anything." One seems like a lonely number until considering the following: From one olive tree came the olives that made the oil used to anoint David king of Israel. By slinging one smooth, small rock that was picked up among thousands in a dry river bed, a giant (Goliath) was destroyed and a nation was liberated from a tyrant. From one tree branch, someone carved the rod Moses carried and was used to bring plagues on Egypt, open the Red Sea, and bring water gushing forth from a rock, fresh water that sustained Israel for forty years. From one seed came a tree that was cut to form the cross that Christ hung on. His death on that cross would defeat the kingdom of darkness, liberate sinners, and bring eternal life for all who would believe on him. Just one seed! When Peter wanted to walk on water, Christ said one word...just one. He said, "Come" (Matt. 14:29). Faith in *one word* sent a man doing something considered insane in the natural sense: stepping out on water in the middle of a deep lake without a lifejacket. One word temporarily defied the law of gravity and upheld a full-grown man as he walked on the water. It was only one word. The name of Jesus is just one word, yet all power is given that name, both in Heaven and on Earth (Matt. 28:18). One word is more important than you think.

Herein is another spiritual principle. God only needs one obedient person to turn around a person, a city, or a nation. Jonah was one prophet sent to Nineveh. The large city heard Jonah's warning, repented, and was spared for many more years. Daniel interpreted one dream and was exalted to a high position in Babylon. And Joseph, himself a dreamer, was gifted to interpret the mysterious symbolism in a spiritual warning; by interpreting Pharaoh's dreams, he prepared for a seven-year famine, saving Egypt and the people of the world, as well as his own family from perishing in Canaan Land.

You are only one person, but God only needs *one person* to make a difference. You may be limited, but with God, you are *unlimited!*

CHAPTER EIGHT

THROUGH A MIRROR, DARKLY

For now, we see only a reflection as in a mirror;
then we shall see face to face. Now I know in part;
then I shall know fully, even as I am fully known.

1 Corinthians 13:12

W E ALL HAVE mirrors in our homes or apartments. The worst time to look into one is when you just get out of bed. I've looked in the mirror and thought, "I could play a role in a horror movie the way I look right now!" Yet, 30 minutes later (yes, I can get ready that fast) I look and say, "Who is that fine-looking fellow in the mirror!" Well, maybe I don't think it quite like that, but you get the point. Maybe it is better said this way—the mirror lies!

According to a study on body wash from Skinbliss, an organization from the U.K., the average woman will spend a total of 136 days getting ready. This includes showers, make-up, choosing the proper clothing, and other various details required to prepare the face and body for public appearances. This translates into 3,264 hours during an average woman's lifetime. Others suggest the actual total time in a girl's lifetime is more like 3 years.

The fact is the mirror is both our best friend and our worst enemy. The reflection is our foe when our early morning twin looks back at us with twisted bed hair, pale face with the unwanted bags laying like tiny deflated balloons under our eyes, and of course all those small blemishes (imperfections on steroids) that capture our attention like dots from a black marker. Then for the more mature among us, there are the droops, sags, and wrinkles that remind us that in the past 8 hours we have somehow been falling apart while lying in a bed.

Within 30 minutes to 1 hour, the same mirror has become our most-appreciated, silent friend. It can't compliment, talk back, encourage or rebuke: but it really doesn't need to because we do all of that to ourselves. The new reflection tells a different story. The *sags* and *bags* have been covered by a new set of clothes, specially designed to hide those unwanted love handles and rolls of flesh that just love your waist line—evidence of too many cakes and pastries. However, the hair now looks great: combed, curled, gelled, and sprayed with the finest hair care products. Now, no one will ever see those facial blemishes as the latest makeup has been smoothed over to hide them, almost like an eraser removing unwanted pencil marks from a piece of paper. You look once from the front, twice from both sides, and finally over your shoulder to check out the posterior. The mirror now tells you how goodlooking you are. There is just one major problem: *The mirror lies!* Let me explain.

When you look into a mirror in the morning, you will always be reminded of something about yourself that you just do not like. If you are short, you wish you were taller; if you are very tall you'd like to have a few inches of height removed. If you have black hair, you wonder what you would look like with blond and, at times the blondes really like the dark-haired look. If you have straight hair, you wish you had a few curls; but that wavy hair is such a pain at times so you spend time with a hot iron to get the waves out! Your nose is too big, your mouth droops too much—you look like you're frowning all the time. And then, there are those eyes—they are dark but blue would surely look better! Don't even bring up the neck down: The hips are too wide, the stomach is too fat, and the other parts just aren't what they should be. After all, look at the people in those magazines at the food checkout lines. Now that's what I should look like…. right?

Well, if you had a plastic surgeon, a fully paid personal trainer to inspire you each morning to exercise, a personal chef that cooks only the healthiest food, and a personal masseuse, then perhaps you could look like a Hollywood star! There is only one major problem with this type of "plastic person." As one man said, "When the Lord returns and all of the plastic falls off, you may not know the person when they arrive in Heaven!" Another point: There is only so much skin that can be trimmed away, pulled up, and tucked into the corner. Time will eventually meet age and the wrinkles will begin sneaking up like unwanted drips in a leaky faucet. The fact is the mirror is constantly lying.

So how is a mirror lying? First, there is much more to beauty than the skin tone and the fleshly body you are living in. Our culture has spent millions of dollars on television commercials and advertisements in magazines, over-emphasizing the need of being slim, trim, and beautiful. Moreover, the implication is that if you can achieve the proper combination, then your perfect looks can take you anywhere, opening doors and making you happy. If this theory were true, then the "happiest" people in the world should be living in Hollywood, as they can afford all of the physical "perks" to make a person go from a "7" to a "10" on the beauty scale. However, why are so many famous people divorcing all the time if *outward beauty* is supposed to be the road to contentment?

What about lots of money? Isn't that supposed to make a person happy? The same deception occurs with money. The perception is that lots of money will make you very happy. If this is true, why do rich people often become alcoholics, drug addicts, and even take their own lives?

Second, what we see in the mirror is not the *real* "us." The Scripture teaches that every human is a tri-part being, consisting of a body, soul, and spirit (1 Thess. 5:23). We see only one part of a three-part person—the physical body. This is the world we live in: a physical world dominated by five physical senses, and our battles with the flesh are all part of the physical realm. However, what about the inside of each person—the soul and the spirit? We are actually an eternal spirit with a soul that is living in a body! The "real you" is not what you see in the mirror. A person can cover their blemishes with makeup and fake out a television viewer who comments on what a "great complexion" she has! However, the real you is not what you see in the mirror.

It is your *personality*, your *compassion*, your *ability to love*, how you *treat others*, and *the loyalty* you have as a friend that is the "real you." When people ask what they think of a certain person, you seldom hear someone say, "Wow, they are sooooo beautiful," or "I just love to look at them!" The comments 99% of the time are "They have a great personality...they are a great worker.... they get along with others well.... they never complain.... you can trust them with anything...they are fun to be with...they love people and it shows." Hey, what happened to the person in the mirror? We spend 1 hour getting ready for work — which is fine and dandy—but our outward appearance is not what co-workers, church members or even family members will remember when they mention your name. It is how you build relationships and your loyalty as a friend.

SEE WHAT GOD SEES

In Heaven, the throne of God sits upon a "sea of glass like a crystal" (Rev.4:6). There is a continual reflection of the glory and presence of God that can be seen on the crystal floor. It is not the physical woman or man that is as important as the inner you that is reflected among others when you leave the room of mirrors and walk among hurting people. Trust me, their interest in you is not the amount you spend on your clothes, the type of makeup, or style of your hair but how much you care.

The mirror is not your true reflection—it is Christ in you that is your true reflection. I think I need to tell you now that there is no reason to get depressed or discouraged when you start getting older, and grey-headed, putting on weight, and slowing down.

All of these will eventually happen to you. I can remember sitting in a church in Baton Rouge, LA, when I realized things were a bit blurry in the distance. I found out I needed glasses, but that was fine because most people look good or even smarter in glasses! Years later, I noticed I would get a bit tired after eating and, after blood tests, was told I am a diabetic. Now that wasn't good news, as my dad passed away at age 78 battling diabetes. I started seeing grey hair in my forties, but read in the Bible that a white head was a crown of glory (Prov. 16:31). So, I said to myself, "God must be making me more glorious in his sight." Then I saw wrinkles under my eyes and was a bit frustrated with that, until I heard a group of people talking about how "distinguished" men look with some wrinkles on their face. Of course, the people saying that were all using some sort of face creams, trying to tighten the bags under their eyes! Finally, I came to this conclusion: My wife Pam thinks I look good, she loves me, therefore who really cares about someone else's opinion!

BUT I AM UGLY

Why do we think we are ugly? Because we compare ourselves to someone else. Guys who may not be athletic or built like a mini-tank often feel inferior. However, macho-boy is not what a mature girl actually desires in life, as macho will over the years "muncho" on chips and cake and become a mucho out of shape honcho! The two top characteristics a mature girl desires in a man are his ability to bring security to her life (provide for her) and his loyalty to her alone. And fellows, you don't have to be a stud-muffin and look like you walked out of a GQ magazine to hook a great woman of

God in your future. Be honest, caring, and understanding—listen more than you speak and she will walk into your life.

Because of peer pressure young girls can become obsessed with their bodies. Some girls struggle with anorexia, an eating disorder in which a person loses their appetite, and characterized by a desire to lose weight. This obsession to be tiny and without any body fat can become a dangerous obsession that leads to an individual actually starving themselves. Obsessions such as these are the devil's tactic to fool you into thinking you should be something that you are not. Instead, become obsessed with the Word.

I realize there is pressure from all directions to have the "perfect body." However, I am going to say something here that I have at times stated in public when preaching on marriage. My precious wife is 5'4" and I am 6'1" or so. From the time we were married, Pam has said she has always struggled with her weight—as many men and women both do. I have seen her lose up to 40 pounds but gain it back, and repeat this cycle several times over the years. She is not so much concerned about how she looks but wants to be healthier.

Here is my point: I like some weight on my sweetie, or as I have told her all our marriage, "I like some chunky on you!" Personally, I could have never married a girl who was thin as a toothpick. That's just me. I actually think that a little weight looks good. Pam says I am a very strange man to feel that way, but I am totally honest. So, my precious wife admits she has struggled with her weight, but to me she is very cute. I like everything about her and to me, her weight is just fine. I am saying that to tell you no matter how you perceive yourself, there will be someone who will love you *just as you are!*

When Pam and I were married in 1982, the traditional Pentecostal church asked women not to wear makeup (of course that has changed—aren't you glad?). My sweetheart did not wear any makeup per-se, but she looks like an angel in my book. When I would wake up beside her in the morning, I always said, "I am married to an angel!"

A natural mirror cannot look into your heart, soul or spirit, as only God can do this. The real you is the inner you and the real me is my "inner me." I may not be the best-looking cookie on the tray, but at least I'm on the tray!

It is difficult to feel good when you feel bad about yourself. There are some things we can change that may help you feel more confident, if these changes do not compromise your faith or walk with God. I remember one girl who battled her weight continually and this depressed her. She made up her mind to work out, watch her eating habits, and over time lost weight. Her transformation was amazing! She feels better physically and her self-confidence has been boosted. What abides in your heart (your faith, hope and love) are far greater that what you see in the mirror as the real you is the inner you.

CHAPTER NINE

DISABILITIES DO NOT MAKE YOU WEIRD

T HE TITLE OF this chapter is not just for anyone who is "different", as it is actually describing myself. Allow me to explain:

First, while growing up into my teenage years and beyond, I noticed several things about me that were very different from the majority of youth my age:

- I was a loner and enjoyed being by myself, needing no friends in the room when I was alone.

- I could not make friends easily as I was quite aloof, with only a few people I considered friends.

- I became stressed every time I had to talk to people I did not know and always said very little in a crowd.

- I did not enjoy going out with people I did not know, only close friends.

- When sitting beside someone I didn't know on a plane, I would fake sleep to avoid speaking.

- For many years (until I was married), I fought depression in some form almost daily.

I began preaching full time when I was 18; thus, I was driving by myself all across the southeastern United States. For many years, I would stay in the pastor's home during the revivals where I preached nightly in the church. One of my earliest revivals in Montcalm, West Virginia, went nightly for three weeks. Many years later, the pastor remembered that during those entire three weeks I stayed in the bedroom praying and studying, never coming out to eat a meal. I was fasting quite a bit but, believe it or not, I was so "shy" that I didn't want to sit at the table and talk. I would rather eat nothing than have to talk to someone!

I realize that there are many people like myself, young and old, who are "shy," and do not enjoy being a "social butterfly"—smiling, laughing, and sharing stories while telling everyone how great they are. For many years, I assumed that this was just my personality, and I knew it would be very difficult for me to change. I was called to preach when I was 16 and began traveling full time at age 18. I can recall I was always a bit nervous and apprehensive when staying in a person's home I did not know. This caused me to book the same churches for revival consecutively year after year, as I was familiar with those people and did not have to go through the process of becoming acquainted with new people.

It would be many years later, in fact when I was in my late forties, that I began to research certain types of autisms, including one called Asperger syndrome. This syndrome is a neurobiological disorder on the higher-functioning end of the autism spectrum and can range from mild to severe. Those with this type of autism exhibit deficiencies in social and communication skills. This is an important fact. Those with the disorder can often become the target for bullying, as individuals may not understand the mannerisms or personality of a person with Asperger. After doing a special test, I discovered that I had a mild level of this type of autism, especially in the area of social skills and communicating to a person one on one. To me, this is a total mystery. I can stand before a massive crowd, preach, teach, and even pray for them. However, once I am finished I prefer to go to my office alone and not be disturbed. If I enter a room, I tend to be drawn to the people I have known for a long time, more than those with whom I have no relationship. When it comes to talking at a table with people I don't know, I can at times find it actually slightly painful to build on a conversation. For me to be alone all day without anyone around does not bother me in the least bit.

After understanding why at times I was a social recluse and why my brain's neurons fired a particular way, I actually laughed at myself. Having the desire to live the life of a "social monk" like a man in a monastery can be viewed as a negative, especially when my life and ministry revolves around ministering to people.

However, *one area* stands out with the majority of individuals who deal with this spectrum of autism, and that is they can become easily preoccupied with a particular subject in exclusion to all others. They also love to amass facts and information. Most have a normal to superior IQ. When I discovered this fact, the light came on in my head and something made total sense for the first time.

I have one area where I am preoccupied with a particular subject. In fact, I have spent over 140,000 hours of my life, studying literally every day since I was called into ministry, on this subject: the Bible. Thus, what would be perceived by outsiders as a strange "social weakness", that would hamper my ability to deal with people one on one and face to face, has one major positive side, and that is the ability to spend entire days on the subject of biblical revelation and information.

People often say to me, "How in the world do you find the time to do all that you have done." My answer is, "I seldom hang around people during the day!" I have written over 60 books, published a magazine for over 30 years, prepared messages for service, and articles for the internet. All of this cannot be done without spending more time with God than with people—and I am very happy to do so!

In my earlier years I heard other young people in public school say to me, "Man, you are weird." I admit I was different, but I was not weird. The word different means "not the same as another," so in that sense we are all different! Just as no two snowflakes are alike, no two people have the same fingerprints, footprints, or patterns in the eyes. Another definition of different means "distinct"; we are all distinct in our own ways. Can you imagine the war between women that would erupt if they all had the same hair color, style, and cut; the same eye color and skin complexion; same weight and height; and the same accent when they talked! I just can't see a female from New York talking like a southern girl and a southerner with the accent of someone from Boston!

Next time someone calls you "weird," remember this: in the old Scottish language, the word "weird" referred to a person's destiny! So when they say, "You are weird," answer, "That's true...I have a destiny!" I am sure they will be a bit confused at your answer.

IT IS NOT THAT STRANGE

The following are really not that strange and may be a part of your personality:

1. To enjoy being alone

There is a difference in being alone because you are depressed and being alone because you enjoy the solitude. Isolation and solitude are two different parts of the spectrum. Isolation is willingly shutting yourself away from family and friends, refusing their concern or interest in some negative situation. Isolation gives you way too much time meditate on your problems, only adding to the weight of oppression you may be experiencing. Solitude, however, is a biblical principle, as often the prophets (and Christ) would separate from the multitudes to spend time alone with God. Isolation places the emphasis on you, but solitude places the emphasis on God.

Many times in the Bible when men were "alone," they received a unique word or visitation from God.

If you are rather shy and prefer to be alone, you are not weird.

2. To Not Want to Do What Others Do

You are not weird if you have no desire to do what others are doing. When you get a call that everyone is going out to eat, headed to a movie, going to the beach, or having a party at someone's house, and you choose not to be involved, never wallow in self-pity as to why you have no desire to do what others do. I attended High School in Salem, Virginia, and having been called to preach at age 16 meant that from tenth grade until graduation, I felt a need to separate myself from others and live a different type of life with Christ. I was the guy who dressed up a bit, carrying a large Dake's Bible to school every day. I could be found reading my Bible at the lunch table while others just laughed, stared, or glared at me. I loved sports, especially football. However, my desire for the Word and presence of God was so intense that I was uninterested in any school event. I can recall only having four people that I considered friends in the entire school! Strangely, that never once bothered me. I figured that God and I made the majority, and if He was for me, then who could be against me.

3. Spend More Time with God than People

One day at OCI, two young men stepped on the property. I recognized one as the son of a missionary we had supported and the other was his cousin. They had "hopped a train" (which is illegal, by the way) and were planning on stopping for a few days then heading toward the Virginia mountains. Both were so high they were in la-la land, but could at least carry on a conversation. I told them they were going to stay in Cleveland, and I was going to mentor them in the Lord (when I had time). I gave them a library of books and some Bibles to read. They spent months reading, and eventually began praying every day. As the revelation of God's Word came alive in their spirit, they began maturing in the Word and now at times spend hours in prayer each day. Today they work with the ministry and continue to pray, and are looking to hit the mission field and evangelize one day!

I told them what one of my mentors, Floyd Lawhon, told me: To be effective in the kingdom, you must spend more time with God than you do with man. They took that advice and began spending every available moment either in prayer or in learning something in the Word that they would use in their lives.

When you love a person, you will love spending time in their presence. Your time with the Lord indicates the level of love you have for Him and His presence. Everything about God centers on relationship. He is a Father; we are His children. Christ is a bridegroom; we are His bride. To build a relationship requires one-on-one time, and intimacy with the one you love. I enjoy playing worship music while driving my car down mountain roads and just talking to the Lord as if He is in the front seat. In the office I always keep music playing as it creates an atmosphere. At times, I suddenly sense the presence of the Lord and I will stop what I am doing, worship, and cry or begin praying intently. We can all pray, and prayer can be alone or in a large group. However, to hear, we must become still and learn to listen.

DON'T LET DISABILITIES STOP YOUR DESTINY

Perhaps you have never heard of Helen Keller. Born in 1880 in Tuscumbia, Alabama, she was born with the ability to see and hear; but at 19 months, she contracted a disease that left her both blind and deaf. Despite her adversity, she learned how to communicate using signs with her hands and fingers. She had to be taught by a teacher writing the names of various objects. Because of her determination, at age 24 she became the first blind and deaf person to earn a Bachelor of Arts degree and she met such noted people as Mark Twain, one of her greatest admirers. In later years, she went on to become a world-renowned speaker and author, writing twelve books and numerous articles. In 1964, President Johnson awarded her the Presidential Medal of Freedom. Who would have believed that a young girl, who was blind and deaf, could accomplish so much and make such an impact upon others? She did not allow her physical limitations to limit her ability to think, reason, plan, and speak.

This woman is one example of many that could be given of those who did not allow physical limitations to limit her ability to expand life beyond the limitation. My bit of autism has provided me with the ability to be alone and study in offices, hotel rooms, and churches for over 140,000 hours! Use what others consider your disadvantage for your advantage, for you can do all things through Christ who gives you the strength (Phil 4:13).

CHAPTER 10

DANGERS WHEN YOU SHOW AND TELL

W HEN I WAS a small chap in elementary school, there was one day of the year called "Show and Tell." The idea was to bring a unique object to school and share an interesting story connected with that object. There were some interesting "things" presented and some rather strange stories told. I am sure some of the stories were embellished a bit to impress the gullible, young minds glued to the speaker as though spellbound. When my brother Phillip, was in first grade and his time came to tell a story, he told a "big one." That same day I received a visit from his teacher, as the entire classroom was upset, crying and wanting to go home to see their parents. My brother had heard me tell some kids in the neighborhood the story about the car wreck I was in with Mom and Dad when I was about 3 years old. I made sure to emphasize the point that we could have all been killed! My little brother was listening and wanted to tell his classmates, but when he told it, he added his own touch, saying that his mom and dad had been tragically lost in the wreck! With the class upset, his teacher called me out of my classroom, into the hallway to privately confirm the authenticity of this sad event. What I related was the same narrative, repeated with the exception of the climax: my parents survived along with myself. That day, "show and tell" had turned into a real "tall tale," an exaggeration that caused a near classroom crisis.

Every day, young people are "showing and telling" far too much, creating possible dangerous situations for themselves. This unlimited release of visual and written information is being published to various forms of social media, including Facebook, Instagram, and other forms of wireless communication. Originally, these formats were message-centered, accessed and viewed when typing in a few words or sentences. Progressively, technology enabled pictures and videos, made visible to anyone wishing to view them, to travel across internet lines and satellites.

Obviously, social media can be used for good and bad, positive and negative purposes. However, here is an example of an unforeseen "negative" response from a Facebook video. Following one of our main youth events at OCI, the Spirit of God came upon a youth group from Florida and they ended up outside, under the front entrance awning, praying and rejoicing, and some lying on their faces or backs under the power of God. Some were so caught up in the Spirit they appeared to be "drunk" (like those on the Day of Pentecost – see Acts 2). My daughter was both thrilled and fascinated and began innocently filming this amazing outpouring. Later, she posted it on a personal page for her friends from OCI to see, all of whom would totally understood what was transpiring. However, she failed to keep it from being reposted to anyone and everyone who could see it. A few Holy Spirit-haters took the video, posted it on their sites and began mocking them, calling the kids demon-possessed, evil, and wicked. There were millions of views and hundreds of comments were horrible. She was distraught and embarrassed, and I told her the spiritual principle here is, you "don't cast your pearl [what is precious] before swine [unbelievers]" (Matt. 7:6). What was precious to her was crazy to someone else, as the carnal mind cannot understand the things of the Spirit of God (1 Cor. 2:14). Posting this to the general may not have been "dangerous", but it was not "wise." There are times however, when what we show and tell can be dangerous.

Security experts warn that when a family is away for vacation, it is not wise to post on Facebook or any public social media that you are going to be out of town. They advise that many home bur-glaries are initiated by thieves who monitor social media to deter-mine when a family is out of town, then break in according to the family's travel schedule. Our home was broken into in the late 1980s. We had a phone with a message recorder to capture the missed calls when we were traveling. The police officer said, "Get rid of that. If they know your phone number they will call, and if they keep getting this recording to leave a message, they will know you are not home." The same is true with newspapers piling up in the driveway or the lights being out all the time at night. These are "thief signals" indicating that no one is at home.

I realize that today's technology enables a person to post only to friends, but many parents are, in my opinion, unwise to post pictures of their children on a page that is accessible to anyone; and parents do this without thinking. The danger is that in every town, there are sex offenders who can prey on children, and the internet is used as the main resource for collecting pictures and personal data. I am not trying to overdramatize this, but kidnappings and sexual assaults have occured because too much was "shown" and "told" on social media.

THE SHOW NEVER GOES AWAY

Technology changes every 3 months, and new devices are introduced every year. Your newest iPhone will be outdated soon, your iPad will need updating, and new, must-have apps will be released. The old will go away and the new will rise to the top—until the next new thing emerges from the tech world. However, some things will literally never go away and that includes some of your show and tell information. Let's say you take a really provocative picture and send it to your "boyfriend." He sees it then deletes it. The fact is it may be deleted from his phone but with cloud storage and the latest government and phone company technologies, it can be stored permanently. This is one way the government can go back in time after a crime to pull down all e-mails, text messages, and pictures in a Federal Case if they have a court warrant to do so. At times, someone in Hollywood wants to "blackmail" another person and old pictures suddenly appear in public, to the horrible embarrassment of the person who for years had thought they'd "disappeared." There have been countless cases in which a girl sent a boy private pictures of herself in a compromising posi-tion, and the boy would resend the picture to his friends or show it to other guys at school, ruining the reputation of the girl as she walks the halls in embarrassment. In the past, some kids have committed suicide because of pictures and text messages that were made public. Just remember, because it was erased does not mean it actually "goes away." What you show and tell on social media can be stored, hacked, and exposed to others.

THE CRITICISM TRAIN

Bullying is very common on social media, and this too has caused heartache and grief for young people who, in their minds, con-nect personal self-esteem to what they perceive others their age think about them. A person will check their "likes" or "dislikes," reminding me of a politician checking his percentages in the morning. I have a Perry Stone Ministries Facebook page, which has about 330,000 people that can see our videos and posts. When I post anything, and I mean *anything*, there is always a majority of positive comments, but at times up to 10 percent will be very neg-ative and hateful in nature. Years ago, I would focus on the nega-tive comments and scratch my head trying to figure out why they were upset with me. Over time, I learned that a person's comment was just that person's opinion, and opinions are like a person's nose — everybody has one! My favor with God, His blessings, and any success I have has *no link at all* to some negative person who doesn't like me, as my blessings are not coming from *their opinion* of me but of *God's opinion* of me. The craziest aspect about people commenting on a Facebook video or picture is that nobody asked for their opinion, yet they are giving it!

Here's some good advice for Facebook critics always giving your negative "opinion." At times, it is better just to close your mouth and not to speak or respond, making people wonder if you're a fool, than to open your mouth, write a comment, and prove it! It is far better to give a person a piece of your heart and love them than a piece of your mind and despise them. Some critics are so negative that even the dog runs in the opposite direction when it sees them coming. There are positive types of criticism that used to correct a situation or expose something that is going to be a trap or danger for you; this is "corrective criticism." However, "abusive criticism" is destructive, not constructive, causing anxiety, depression, and rejection among some youth.

Often there is a root cause as to why some people are critical of others, as there is something about you for them to be jealous of (looks, possessions, etc.). Jealousy is a feeling of resentment toward another person, causing them to put down that person verbally. Someone who is always clipping other people's wings is usually a person who can't fly. If they can't have something, then they don't want you to have it either. If they aren't as smart as you are, they will call you dumb. If they have little finances and you are financially blessed, then you are selfish and greedy. If you have many friends and they don't, then you are arrogant. If you are spiritual, then you are a hypocrite or a religious freak. If you have a car and they have to be driven to school, then you are a spoiled brat. These are statements from a resentful and perhaps hurting person. Jesus taught we should pray for those who say spiteful things against us

(Matt. 5:44), as they need God to touch their heart and there is no edification in arguing with them. Perhaps one of the greatest quotes I ever read that sum up critical people is this: "I have been all over the world and have never seen a monument or statue of a critic" (Leonard Bernstein).

I have plenty of critics. If a close friend who loves me tries to correct me and I need it, I listen. If a person I have no relationship with trash talks me, I just ignore it. I compare an abusive and opinionated critic to something I saw in West Virginia. My Granddad Stone lived near a railroad track. Several times a day a train would rumble down the tracks, shaking his house like a mini-earthquake. One day I saw a stray dog sitting near the tracks as though waiting for the train. He would stare in one direction. Suddenly you could feel the train coming, and the little fellow sprung to all fours. He hunched over glaring at the direction of the train. The moment the train rounded the bend, he began barking wildly until the engine drowned him out. Then, he began running beside the train. I could see his mouth moving, nipping at the base of the round metal wheels. What was funny, the engineer never saw the dog, the train was certainly not impacted, yet this little mutt must have felt he was some big dog battling the huge train. The thought came to me, "The dog barks and the train rolls on!" I use this to illustrate how bullies, critics and negative people are just like a snappy little dog whose bark is worse than their bite. You are on the Gospel Train with the Lord and you are rolling toward your assignment, your job, or your ministry. Just let the critics bark and let the train roll on.

ARE YOU ADDICTED TO SOCIAL MEDIA?

Social media can certainly be used as an effective tool for ministry and a resource to keep friends and family updated. However, it is possible to become "hooked" to our phones and computers in a dangerous manner. My wife Pam wrote an article about social media in our VOE magazine that I want to place in this section. Warning: It might sting a bit but it is true. It is titled, "Are you Addicted to Social Media?"

It seems every person, even the youngest children, are walking around with a cell phone 'stuck' to their hand, or protruding from their jean pockets. It reminds me of the old Wild West movies, where every man is strutting down the dirt street with a six-shooter holstered on their hip. Their weapon was inseparable, attached when riding their horse, when sitting at a table, when walking down the sidewalk, and was laid to rest at night beside their dresser—always within hand's reach. To some girls, keeping their phone connected to their bodies is more important than wearing make-up and fixing their hair! However, there is a genuine concern that this generation has become *addicted* to the social media craze and to electronic relationships.

A drug or alcohol addict convinces themselves that they cannot survive without a "drink" or a "fix." They literally thrive for the next high or "buzz" from some substance that they believe is needed for their daily survival. Tell them to go one day without feeding their addiction and they believe they could die. Some would fight you to keep their daily pattern from collapsing for even one day. If you believe I am exaggerating, just ask any former drug addict who once felt their existence was dependent upon some chemical or alcohol high.

Sociologist and psychiatrists are now greatly concerned that this "social media generation" has become so addicted to the apps, pictures, texts, and information, that they are becoming functionally dysfunctional, meaning they can multi-task on the latest iPhone but are socially dysfunctional. I have seen a group of youth sit at a table in a fast food joint, all glued to their phone screens, and not carry on one normal conversation between each other. Some can sit for 30 minutes, literally never looking up once to speak as they chomp on a greasy burger with one hand and continually slide their thumb across the phone screen with the other. When their ring tone pierces the air, nothing else matters as they reach for their phone, interpreting the latest text abbreviations or laughing at someone's latest "selfie" picture.

Here are the facts. The average person spends 8 hours and 41 minutes on electronic devices. Four in ten people check their phones at night if it wakes them. According to *The Daily Mail*, the average person checks their phone 110 times a day! People average receiving 22 phone calls a day and send or receive messages 23 times a day — and these are mostly personal calls and messages. Every six and one half minutes, people are looking at their phones!

Texting while driving or looking at a video while behind the wheel has caused deadly accidents. The National Safety Council said that 1.6 million car crashes occur each year because a person was on their cell phone. Also, 330,000 injuries occur each year from accidents caused by texting and driving. In the United States, 1 in 4 accidents are caused by texting and driving. It takes 5 seconds to read a text when driving, and if you are going 55 MPH these 5 seconds are equal to traveling the length of a football field. If someone suddenly switches lanes or puts on their brakes, you are in serious trouble. Here's what is illogical: 77% of young adults think they can safely text and drive! The stats show that teens who text and drive spend 10% of drive time over the line in the other lane of traffic when texting. What's even more insane is 1 in 5 youth actually surf the web while driving. I hate to admit it but if you are part of that group, you are addicted to your phone like an addict is drugs. This activity has rewired our brains and caused many to have a serious attention disorder.

Seriously, no wonder most Christians can't pray longer than five minutes at a time, as our brain is programmed to stop and check out the phone every six minutes. In the past, the average "prayer break," when a person started praying and then went back to their pew, from the church altars occurred every 13 minutes—the average break time between television commercials as a commercial break averages every 13 minutes! People watch an average of 8 hours of television daily, and the brain became accustomed to the 13-minute-get-up-and-take-a-break-then-come-back routine. Perry has observed for years Christians who kneel at the altar, pray intently for an average of 13 minutes, then get up *all at the same time* about 12 to 13 minutes after praying, returning to their seats! The pre-television generation of the 1960s could pray for hours, and today the continual television-watching generation prays an average of 13 minutes, if that much. Now, prayer time is reduced to an average of only 5 minutes because our brain waves are signaling, "Its check the phone time." Yes, electronic devices have seriously rewired our brains, and our spiritual lives are feeling the effects of it! People can no longer exercise on a treadmill without watching the news, listening to music, or having a screen in front of them. In reality, the brain needs some down time just to relax, but instead it is being flooded continually with messages, voices, moving screens and endless images. Researchers are saying there is *electronic fatigue* actually occurring in the brain, but instead we are so interactive with social media the brain has little time to actually process all the downloads flooding the neurons.

Facebook, Twitter, Periscope, and other social media can keep a person within fingers reach of someone's personal life. Honestly, even adults become ridiculous with this process. They let people know, "I am now shopping at Food Lion," or, "I'm now drinking my latte at

Starbucks." I am honestly surprised they are not telling you every time they take a restroom break, tweeting, "I am now headed to the restroom!" Friend, I have far too many important things that impact my life and family than to follow a Facebook addict, or a reality television wannabe.

Chick-fil-A had a great idea. The company initiated a "family challenge" asking customers to put their cell phones on silent and place them in a "Cell Phone Coop" until their meal is over. If you make it through the meal without using your phone, you are rewarded with free ice cream. There was great success with the test, proving it is possible to have a meal and enjoy normal conversations while your phone receives a needed break from you.

Why not take a break from social media and see how well you actually do? This includes cutting off the television, putting away phones at mealtime and not getting on the computer, but talking a walk, going to the mall, or better yet, getting still and hearing from the Lord. Go outside, sit in the sun and just pray a while. If we spent even one tenth of the time in prayer that is wasted on useless social media, we might see a sudden revival break out.

Think about it! Today, it is virtually impossible to live a private life as everything seems to be recorded, taped, videoed on security cameras, or stored on hard drives. Your best alone time will be between you and God, and there is no necessity of any electronic device when communicating directly with your heavenly Father.

Put away the gadgets and turn off the electronic hindrances, and get some real "one on one face time" with God. It will truly change your life.

CHAPTER 11

THE BULLY ON THE PLAYGROUND

I F YOU HAVE never been verbally or physically harassed or "bullied," consider yourself quite fortunate. When a young person is bullied in school, it impacts everything. They can lose their desire to attend school or go to class, and it may also impact their grades and their social skills. I know all too well about being bullied and the mental intimidation and emotional stress it creates.

Unless your parents are in the military or the ministry, or move due to a divorce or career change, most youth can settle down with their family or guardian in the same town, attending the same school district from kindergarten through graduation. This makes it a bit easier when you can attend classes with many of the same friends for twelve years. I was not that "fortunate," as I had to change schools four different times.

I began my academic education from Kindergarten through

fourth grade in Big Stone Gap, Virginia. Dad was then asked to pastor a church in Arlington, Virginia. The family moved from a small, rural town, where everyone knew everyone, to a major city where most homes had small or no yards, and continually congested automobile traffic, with different nationalities in every store. It was a culture shock. I discovered that kids were still kids in northern Virginia as they were in the south, with one big exception — there were not nearly as many Christians and church attendees in northeastern Virginia, and few students seemed interested in any discussion concerning "religion" or Christianity. When entering the seventh grade for junior high, I was in for another shock. This was 1972 and these kids in seventh, eighth, and ninth grade were already taking drugs, drinking alcohol, and having sexual relations on the weekends. I also entered what I call "the season of the bullies" as Kenmore Junior High School, where I attended, seemed to have one lurking in every hall. There were a few clashes with boys who thought they were God's gift to girls and so *stuck* on themselves that if they were cremated, you could use them for super-glue.

The following event was so disturbing to me that I can recall the details forty-six years later. It was art class and the teacher had stepped out of the room, leaving the class with a specific assignment. I was rather shy, didn't meet new people very well, and had a major inferiority complex, at times battling depression. On this day, a "bully" came over to me and asked me to stand up. He untied my shoes, and then tied both shoes together. He demanded me to take my buckteeth, make a rabbit face, and hop around the classroom like a rabbit or he would fight me after school. I did as he demanded out of fear as the kids all roared in laughter—all at the expense of my embarrassment and humiliation. He saw the response and released a second demand. He poured paint on a spot and said, "Now, rabbit, lick up that paint." I recall the teacher stepped back in and her presence saved me from further humiliation. This one act lasting about four minutes put a fear and dread in me, and I literally despised going to art class thinking this bully would do this again. At the time, I was a young Christian and at the same time began thinking about how I could defend myself. I decided that if he did this again, I would find something to hit him so hard it would knock him out. I'm glad it never came to that. By ninth grade, I had physically grown up and began playing football. The advantage of joining the football team was that I could meet some of those guys who harassed me years ago and take out my frustration on them in practice—and it was perfectly legal and normal!

Too often, when a person feels bullied, they feel they have no one to turn to who actually understands the fear, frustration, and dread that overwhelms them when they have to see that person, sit in the same class, or continually put up with negative comments. Christian youth should never engage in such foolishness and should find those suffering from this harassment and befriend that person, as many of these individuals just need a true friend. When I hear any of my OCI kids, especially those in a public school, talk about being bullied, in my spirit I can relive the feelings I had in school, and have compassion toward them.

I can remember moving from Arlington to Salem, Virginia during my first year of high school. This was a new place, a new school, and all new people. For weeks, I dreaded to get up and attend school. By now, I was a strong believer and would never compromise my stand with the Lord. I did find a few, and I do mean a few, teens who attended church and a few who were Christians, but they seemed to hide their light and weren't public about their faith. I was not vocal but I carried a black, leather Dake's Bible around all the time, which inspired the students to give me the nick-name, "Preacher man."

On a lighter note, one day a fellow that lived up the street from me approached me walking down the hall and suddenly, without warning, violently shoved me into a locker. He was a rather large fellow and he began pressing his body up against me as if attempting to cause me physical pain. He finally backed up and without thinking, I looked at him and said, "I rebuke you in Jesus name!" He laughed and I repeated it, "I rebuke that spirit in you in Jesus name!" He then stared at me, making some negative comments, and strutted away. That afternoon, I saw him on his motorcycle passing my house and he gave me a gesture with a certain finger.

The next day at school, I was stunned to see both his legs in casts and him hobbling on crutches. He saw me and a look of fear broke over his countenance. He said, "Man, get away from me! What did you do, put a curse on me?" I told him I didn't curse him but did rebuke him for his actions. He said he was riding his motorcycle and after passing my house his cycle went out from under him and tore up his legs. I took time to witness to him, but at the same time, had to laugh within myself thinking, "Man, did the Lord ever silence that bully!"

Years later, in May when graduation day arrived, I recall so many in my senior class being sad, crying, and hugging as one journey in their life ended and another would soon begin. For me, however, I was so relieved and glad school was over so I could be free to travel to churches and preach. I can honestly say there was nothing about public school I missed, as my life had taken an unexpected turn toward a call in the ministry.

Thankfully, today most schools have a no-tolerance policy for bullying and because of horrible circumstances that have occurred to some, there are teachers or counselors in schools that can be approached to address the issue. A victim of bullying can hold in their feelings, move toward isolation, and eventually enter a state of depression that can become dangerous if unchecked.

THE BIBLE'S BIGGEST BULLY

Just the name Goliath sounds intimidating. This man, called a "giant," was a Philistine champion whose height was over ten feet tall. His outward jacket of armor weighed 150 pounds, and his spear was as large as a weaver's beam, which is about 2 ½ inches in diameter, making the spear about twelve feet high with the iron spearhead weighing 18 pounds. Some suggest that Goliath was so large that, to keep from chasing his spear after he threw it, he tied a cord around it that would uncoil when thrown so he could reel it back in to himself (similar to a harpoon used to spear a fish). If he missed once, he would reel it in and thrust the long spear a second or third time.

Goliath was the first "bully" in Scripture and his verbal taunting happened twice a day: in the morning and evening. Oddly, morning and evening were the set times when Jews were to pray. Goliath was interrupting the prayer time of God's people. Just like an uncoiled cord on a spear that is thrown, pulled back and thrown again, bullying is a repetitive act that can happen every time a victim is in the eyesight of the bully, creating a repetitive battle, a struggle that repeats itself over and over again. Victims are caught in a vicious cycle.

Often, the same types of attack can occur but they come at different times. For example, when Jesus refused to submit to Satan's temptations in the wilderness, we read that, "Satan departed [from him] for a season" (Luke 4:13). This meant that Satan left Christ alone for the time being, until down the road at a later point or a more opportune moment, he could hit him again with another form of temptation. It was the same weapon, temptation, but Satan pulled out a different method and used different people.

If you do the same thing again and again you get the same results. At times, getting free from a repetitive cycle of addiction, temptation, or harassment is like climbing a big mountain: It is exhausting. At the same time, the hardest mountain climbing is often climbing out of a rut that we find ourselves in. For example, a repetitive temptation that we submit to or an addiction we are bound in becomes a rut cycle that is difficult to break.

Those who struggle with addictions understand the necessity of breaking the cycle. It actually takes about 18 months in a rehab, away from drugs, pornography, or alcohol, to purge the brain and rewire a person's thinking. The only faster way to slay the addiction or temptation giant is when the supernatural power of God enters the battle; the anointing of the Spirit breaks the bondage and the giant bows to the ground, submitting to the yoke-breaking power of God. There are many people that were under complete control of a goliath-sized bondage, who encountered the delivering power of God in a service and were instantly set free. One of my close friends was a drug dealer and he used illegal drugs. When he came to Christ, the stronghold of drug use was instantly broken and from that moment, for the past thirty years, he has never looked back. He partied hard when he was a sinner and determined to worship and pray as hard as he once partied!

THE MEANING OF GOLIATH'S NAME

The name Goliath is interesting. In Hebrew it comes from a root verb *gala* which means "to uncover" or may also mean "to go into exile." The purpose of Satan's words, negative words from an enemy, or the actions of a bully are spiritually designed to pull you away from faith in God and bring you into exile, or into spiritual and mental bondage. I was bullied in my school days and I experienced a feeling of dread every school day morning when I got up, knowing it could turn into a bad day real fast. When I was a kid in school, there was a saying that "sticks and stones can break my bones but words will never hurt me." After being harassed verbally, I said, "Whoever made up that phrase must have been deaf and could not hear negative words, because mean words, such as 'You are just stupid,' or 'you are ugly,' and 'you're fat,' do hurt." Proverbs 18:8 teaches, "The words of a talebearer are as wounds, and they go down to the innermost parts of the belly."

Goliath was the original biblical bully that intimidated Israel's soldiers so badly that no one wanted to fight him—not one man in the entire Israeli army! David, a teenager at the time, had been worshipping and praying in the Judean mountains, defeating bears and lions, and was not intimidated by the size, the threats, or the weapons of this Philistine bully. Goliath was meant to *intimidate* the men of Israel, and did, until a kid with a fresh anointing showed up with five rocks and a slingshot. Remember, Satan's strategy is to intimidate you, making you back up from your faith and confidence in Christ.

There is an interesting tradition related to David prior to his face-to-face confrontation with Goliath. Jewish tradition says that when David saw and heard Goliath, he first said to himself, "Who can stand against this giant man." Then he heard Goliath curse and blaspheme the name of God. David then said, "I can kill him because he has cursed God and there is no defense or protection around him." In the Law of Moses when a person blasphemed God's name, they broke one of the Ten Commandments (Exod. 20:7), resulting in the death penalty: death by stoning (Lev. 24:10-16). David selected five smooth stones and used the method required by the Law (stoning) to destroy a blasphemer.

Some suggest that the name Goliath can also mean "soothsayer," meaning one that uses words to make predictions. In 1 Samuel 17, Goliath predicted he would defeat anyone in Israel. Morning and night, he predicted he would feed their carcasses to birds of the air, harassing the Israeli army camped across the valley. The enemy is always planting negative, discouraging words in your mind attempting to beat you down spiritually.

The narrative of David and Goliath is important because David was just a teenager (17 or 18) when he stood face to face with a guy twice his size. David was the youngest in the family, thus not old enough to be in the army, as men had to be 20 years of age to enter military service (see Num. 1:3). Although by the Law of Moses he was too young to fight, David had several older brothers serving in the Israeli military. When he showed up on the battlefield his older brother Eliab said, "I know the pride and the naughtiness of your heart. You have come down to watch the battle" (1 Sam. 17:28). It appears that David's brother confused David's *confidence* for *arrogance*, and his *boldness* for *pride*. Don't be surprised that when God begins to bless you as a young person and when His presence is with you, a new confidence and boldness will emerge from your personality. Expect some misunderstanding from other youth that may comment, saying you are "too spiritual," "too religious," and "think you are better" than them. This is just a Goliath smack–talking you, and their opinions need to be ignored. Notice that David did not verbally clash with his brother's jealous comment but replied, "What have I now done? Is there not a cause?" (1 Sam. 17:29).

A bully's words do two things: They *weaken* and they *wound*. In Joshua 7, when Israel went to their second battle they were defeated by men in a small city called Ai. Israel lost no one in battle at Jericho but in this much smaller war, thirty men were slain. We read that the men's hearts in Israel *melted like water* (Josh. 7:5). This indicated they felt weak, which would impact their strength in this war. Negative circumstances weaken, but hateful words also wound, as pointed out in Proverbs 18:8: "The word of a talebearer go down into the innermost parts of the belly." This area of the "belly" is where your eternal spirit is located (see John 7:38 KJV).

When you are in fear or anxiety, you can actually feel the pain in your "belly" or literally in your spirit. Researchers have discovered a "gut nerve" which can actually react to emotions such as fear, anxiety, and stress. Thus, what the ears hear and the eyes see, the brain reads and the nerves of the body actually react to it. The pain a person feels when they sense rejection is not a figment of the imagination, as many suggest. Researchers have discovered that the same brain neurons that signal when a person has been physically hurt also react to emotional hurts in the same manner.

There are physical, spiritual, and emotional hurts. Physical hurt can be a result of accidents and sickness; spiritual hurts are created by various spiritual attacks including jealousy, gossip, unforgiveness and so forth; emotional hurts are often initiated by broken relationships and hurting words. According to recent research, the root cause of hurt is that *we perceive that we have less value with the person or the group than we desire.* We want to be liked, but we perceive we are not. We desire to be accepted in a group, but perceive we are not. We want to feel loved but feel rejection instead. The same neurotransmitters that signal the body is experiencing physical pain are activated during times of emotional rejection or separation. Thus, *rejection creates pain.* One component of the brain gives the location on the body where a physical pain is originating. When pain is linked as an emotional component, a feeling of distress is released to the person experiencing verbal assaults. The physical and emotional feeling of pain is remediated from two different parts of the brain. What researchers learned, is that when a person is hurt by words or actions, the brain indicates that some type of damage is done. Thus, the pain is not a feeling someone is making up in their imagination to receive sympathy or attention but is very real and felt. It must be dealt with through prayer, forgiveness, and allowing the Spirit of God to bring emotional healing.

Some of the most difficult wounds to recover from are when you are wounded in the house of God, the church. Under the direction of Paul, Timothy was a young man pastoring a large church who had to deal with the negative reaction of elders towards his ministry. The older members felt he was too young and inexperienced to pastor such a large congregation. This caused a "spirit of fear" to seize Timothy's mind and intimidate him. Paul reminded Timothy that God did not give him a "spirit of fear," but of "power, love, and a sound mind." He then instructed Timothy to, "Let no man despise your youth" (1 Tim. 4:12), and not to rebuke an older member of the church (1 Tim. 5:1). He told Timothy how to battle this intimidation. Paul had released a personal prophetic word to Timothy concerning his call to the ministry at that particular location and reminded him to fight with the prophecies that went before him (1 Tim. 1:18). He was also instructed to stir up the spiritual gifts that he had allowed to die out or neglect (2 Tim. 1:6). In summary, Timothy was to view his ministry not by what some critics perceived about him but what the Holy Spirit had said about him. He was able to rekindle the vision of his calling and to relight the fire and zeal that he once had. Timothy could have wallowed in self-pity and wrapped himself in the clothing of rejection, but he threw off the garments others were attempting to place over him.

I began evangelizing at age 18, and recall the reaction of some older people in the churches when they learned a teenager was coming to preach. They'd cemented in their minds a pre-conceived idea that a kid preacher could tell them nothing they didn't already know, since they had been saved twice as long as I had been alive. Instead of being intimidated, their attitude inspired me to study longer and harder. I determined that I would learn something new every day during my Bible study and, when preaching, would attempt to teach fresh truths from a Hebraic or historical perspective that were insights not commonly known or taught. Eventually, the older saints were amazed at God's wisdom in the preaching and instead of sitting back with their arms folded, many of them jumped headfirst into the river of revival. Pain can be turned into gain, and negative experiences can become your testimony of victory, if you respond properly.

HOW TO DEAL WITH THE BULLY

When you have someone who seems to target you with their verbal assaults, there are several Biblical and wisdom keys you need to know.

First, if you are being harassed because you are a Christian, then rejoice in it because Jesus said when you are persecuted for him, "rejoice and leap for joy, for great is your reward in Heaven" (Luke 6:22-23). I was once being verbally persecuted for my faith in high school and I looked at the guy and said, "Keep it up you are helping me out!" He looked puzzled and I began laughing. He was increasing my reward in Heaven and didn't know it. Also, remember that any verbal persecution is nothing compared to the harassment and physical torture of Christians arrested in

Communists nations, many beaten for the Gospel and others imprisoned without food. Western believers who have met these individuals say these persecuted saints pray to God, not asking for relief from their tormentors but petitioning God to save their enemies, praying, "Thank you, God, that you have chosen me to be persecuted for your name's sake." Persecution strengthens them instead of weakening them. Never back up from your confession as a Christian in front of others, as Jesus said, "If you deny me before men I will deny you before my Father" and "whoever confesses me before men, I will also confess before the angels" (Matt. 10:33, Luke 12:8).

Second, the Bible teaches us to "pray for those who despitefully use us" (Matt. 5:44). This means that if people verbally, physically, or emotionally abuse a believer, we should not curse them or pray evil upon them, but call out their name and ask God to open their eyes and save them. I know of a situation where a legal team in a certain city came against a local church, attempting to block them from building. The church prayed and years later, the same people who fought them so hard attended that church and are now some of their best members! When I see people who are Christian fighters and Bible haters, who continually nitpick a believer, I see them in my spirit saved and filled with the Spirit. Instead of fighting back, begin to express concern and love to that person. It is hard for them to understand and resist love, and you're also heaping "coals of fire on their head" (Rom. 12:20), meaning that your loving response can make them come under conviction for how they are treating you. So endure the persecution and pray for the persecutor. I know this is difficult, and your flesh wants to make them feel the hurt you are feeling, but this is God's way; imagine your joy if and when they turn to the Lord.

Third, as far as a public school bully, it is best to try to avoid them when possible. However, when the situation becomes intense, then your parents or guardian should be made aware of the situation, along with the proper school authorities. Block the person electronically and contact a legal authority if threats are being made against you on social media or in person. At times, internet threats became reality. Bullied people ignored warnings, only to later regret that action was not taken.

It is also important to remember that you may not know what the bully is dealing with personally. I have known of young men who could be nice to others when they wanted to, but when confronted or told to stop their negative actions, could suddenly go off in a rage and began making threats and horrible statements. After counseling, it was discovered that this is the same way their mom or dad acted toward them at home. Some kids live with abusive, alcoholic, or drug-addicted parents, and their life at home is miserable. They are frustrated and take out their frustration on others, including schoolmates. This is not an excuse releasing them from their actions, but at times, their problem may be deeper than anyone knows. This is where praying for them is very important; so ask God to help them cope with family issues.

In conclusion, never bully a person because of their intelligence, weight, dress, appearance, accent when they speak, or for any other reason. How would you feel if someone pointed you out and began mocking you before others? If you see someone who does not fit in, who perhaps has physical handicaps or other issues, take up for them and be a friend. Your goal should not be popularity with the crowd but obedience to God.

Remember that the beautiful pearl on that expensive necklace was once a parasite or irritant inside an oyster or mussel. The forming of a pearl is an amazing act of nature. The inside of an oyster or mussel shell has mantle tissue concealed within it. A tiny object gains access (or on pearl farms is inserted) to the inside of the shell. The mantle tissue then secretes a substance to begin coating the small agitation; as time passes, layers of this coating cover the tiny parasite or inserted object. After about three to five years, something of great value is formed inside the shell — a beautiful round pearl.

When you are being irritated or agitated, allow the Word of God to coat your mind and spirit, covering (or mantling) the pain and hurt with the life-giving power of the Word and Spirit of God. Eventually, what was intended for your demise will become your testimony, having been transformed into something of great beauty and worth.

CHAPTER 12

CONCLUSION

I HOPE THESE NOTES and nuggets from my journey with God have been an inspiration, and given you some important spiritual and practical truths you can use.

I assume that the majority of the youth (or perhaps adults) reading this book are believer's in Christ and have received him as both Savior and Lord. It is possible there is someone reading, who has not completely dedicated their life to the Lord. According to the Bible, there is one way to eternal life and that is through Jesus Christ (John 14:6). This was the purpose of Christ being born of a virgin (Isa. 7:14; Matt. 1:23) and being crucified, buried and raised from the dead (Matt. 27-28): to bring a covenant of redemption and eternal life to all who would believe on him. Today, Christ is seated on the right of God's heavenly throne, ever living to make intercession for you when you pray (see Heb. 7).

If you have read this book, and have never dedicated your heart and life to Jesus Christ, this is the time. As the Scripture says,

"Now is the day of salvation" (2 Cor. 6:2), meaning do not put this decision of receiving Christ as your Savior off to a future time. Acknowledge you are a sinner, and then ask him to forgive you of your sins, dwell within your heart, and take direction of your life. Once you receive him into your heart and spirit, you must grow in the knowledge of the Bible. Find a good Bible-believing church and begin to find friends and people who will help you grow in the Lord.

When you hear that OCI is hosting an event for youth, you are invited to be a part of the event. When I am ministering in your area, please come out and bring friends! Follow me for written and recorded updates on Perry Stone Ministries Facebook page, on Periscope, Twitter and at perrystone.org.

REMNANT

OCI

OCIMINISTRIES.ORG
FOR MORE INFORMATION

AMERICA'S YOUTH GATHERING!

WARRIOR-FEST

OCIMINISTRIES.ORG
FOR MORE INFORMATION

Release the Roar

CONFERENCES WITH PERRY STONE
VISIT OCIMINISTRIES.ORG FOR MORE INFORMATION

OCIMINISTRIES.ORG
FOR MORE INFORMATION